A Country Store In Your Mailbox®

Gooseberry Patch
600 London Road
P.O. Box 190
Delaware, OH 43015

www.gooseberrypatch.com
1·800·854·6673

Copyright 2006, Gooseberry Patch 1-931890-88-9
First Printing, May, 2006

All rights reserved. No part of this book may be reproduced or utilized
in any form or by any means, electronic or mechanical, including
photocopying and recording, or by any information storage and retrieval
system, without permission in writing from the publisher.

Do you have a tried & true recipe...
tip, craft or memory that you'd like to see featured in a **Gooseberry
Patch** book? Visit our website at **www.gooseberrypatch.com**, register
and follow the easy steps to submit your favorite family recipe.
Or send them to us at:

Gooseberry Patch
Attn: Book Dept.
P.O. Box 190
Delaware, OH 43015

Don't forget to include the number of servings your recipe makes,
plus your name, street address, phone number and e-mail address.
If we select your recipe, your name will appear right along with
it...and you'll receive a **FREE** copy of the book!

Contents

Favorite Fall Sippers 5

Farm-Fresh Breakfasts 25

Hay-Day Appetizers 53

Farmstand-Fresh
Sides & Salads...........................77

Country-Style
Soups & Breads......................109

Slowly-Simmered
Flavors of Fall...................135

A Thankful
Heart...Harvest
Main Dishes 163

Autumn
Treats.............193

Dedication:

For our friends who love sweater weather, this is just for you!

Appreciation:

For your freshly-picked bushel of harvest recipes...we thank you!

Favorite Fall Sippers

Cinnamon-Maple Nog

Kathy Grashoff
Fort Wayne, IN

A yummy beverage for sipping on a chilly evening.

6 c. milk
1 c. maple syrup
2 t. cinnamon

2 t. allspice
Optional: 6 4-inch cinnamon
    sticks

Combine milk and syrup in a saucepan; warm over medium-low heat, until heated through. Stir in cinnamon and allspice; serve hot. Garnish with cinnamon sticks, if desired. Serves 6.

Spicy Citrus Cider

Ellen Folkman
Crystal Beach, FL

Keep this warm in a slow cooker...everyone can help themselves.

8 c. apple juice
2-1/4 c. water
1-1/2 c. orange juice
3 4-inch cinnamon sticks

1 T. whole cloves
1/4 c. molasses
Optional: apple slices

Combine all ingredients except apple slices in a large saucepan over medium heat. Simmer for 10 minutes, stirring occasionally. Strain before serving, if necessary. Garnish with apple slices, if desired. Makes about 3 quarts.

Fireside Sipper

Judy Voster
Neenah, WI

Everyone will welcome a mug of this warm, spicy drink...especially coming in from raking leaves or a country hayride.

4 c. apple juice
1/4 c. brown sugar, packed
6 allspice berries
6 whole cloves

4-inch cinnamon stick
3/4 c. apricot brandy or
apricot nectar
Optional: apple slices

Combine apple juice and brown sugar in a medium saucepan. Simmer over low heat, stirring occasionally, until sugar is dissolved. Tie spices in cheesecloth; add to pan and simmer for 15 minutes. Remove from heat; discard spices. Stir in brandy or nectar. Serve hot in mugs; garnish with apple slices, if desired. Makes 6 servings.

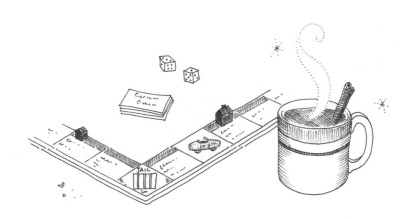

That first crackling fire and scent of wood smoke tells us it's fall! Gather lots of games and puzzles for cozy nights at home with family & friends.

Creamy Sweet Almond Milk

Cathryn Fridell
Orient, OH

Sure to lull you to sleep.

2-1/2 c. milk

1-1/2 T. almond-flavored syrup

Combine milk and almond syrup in a saucepan; heat to desired temperature. Makes 2 servings.

Hot Chocolate Supreme

Lisa Allbright
Crockett, TX

Curl up and enjoy a mug of this chocolatey cocoa.

1 c. sugar
1/2 c. baking cocoa
1/4 t. salt
5 c. water
2 c. milk

1 c. whipping cream
Garnish: marshmallows or
    frozen whipped topping,
    crushed peppermint candies

Combine sugar, cocoa and salt in a saucepan; whisk in water. Bring to a boil over high heat, stirring until sugar is completely dissolved. Reduce heat to medium; add milk and cream. Heat through and keep warm over low heat. Serve topped with marshmallows or whipped topping and sprinkled with crushed peppermint candies. Serves 4 to 6.

Line the mantel with lots of votives tucked inside orange, gold, brown and green votive holders. Surround them with apples, acorns and bittersweet vines.

FAVORITE FALL
Sippers

Mocha Coffee Mix

Melody Taynor
Everett, WA

This mix is sure to be a welcome hostess gift!

2 c. powdered non-dairy creamer   1 t. cinnamon
1-1/2 c. hot chocolate mix   1/2 t. nutmeg
1-1/2 c. instant coffee granules

Sift together creamer, hot chocolate mix, instant coffee, cinnamon and nutmeg; store in airtight container. To use: Stir one tablespoon of mixture into one cup of hot water; adjust to taste. Makes about 5 cups.

Maple Cream Coffee Creamer

Sharon Demers
Dolores, CO

This creamer is good in hot cocoa too!

14-oz. can sweetened   1 t. maple extract
    condensed milk   1 t. vanilla extract
1-1/2 c. milk

Combine all ingredients in a blender; mix until well blended. Pour into a quart-size container; store in refrigerator for up to 2 weeks. Makes about 4 cups.

Ah! There is nothing like staying home for real comfort.

-Jane Austen

Fall Harvest Warmer

Geneva Rogers
Gillette, WY

*Pour into a thermos and tote to a football game...just the thing
for keeping warm on those crisp fall evenings!*

2 c. water
1/2 c. sugar
2 4-inch cinnamon sticks
10 whole cloves

2 c. cranberry juice cocktail
1 c. orange juice
Garnish: orange slices

Combine water, sugar and spices in a saucepan over medium-high
heat; bring to a boil. Add juices; reduce heat and simmer for
10 minutes. Discard spices. Serve warm, garnished with orange slices.
Makes 4 servings.

Keep a warm quilt or blanket-stitched throw in the car for
autumn picnics and football games...perfect for
keeping warm & cozy.

Lemony Ginger Tea

Angie Venable
Gooseberry Patch

Host a tea party for favorite little girls...they will love it!

6 green teabags
6 c. water
4 t. sugar
1-inch piece fresh ginger, peeled
    and thinly sliced

8 strips lemon zest, about
    2-1/2"x1" each
Optional: lemon slices

Place teabags in a teapot; set aside. Combine water, sugar, ginger and zest in a large saucepan. Bring to a boil; reduce heat and simmer, uncovered, for 10 minutes. Strain liquid into teapot, discarding ginger and zest. Cover and let steep until tea is desired strength. Remove and discard teabags; serve immediately. If desired, garnish with lemon slices. Makes 6 servings.

Fill a vintage teakettle with mulling spices and cinnamon sticks, then fill with water. Let it gently simmer on the stove so the sweet fragrance will fill your home.

French Hot Chocolate

Francie Stutzman
Dalton, OH

This is the best hot chocolate I've ever tasted!

2 to 3 1-oz. sqs. unsweetened
   baking chocolate
1/2 c. water
3/4 c. sugar

1/8 t. salt
1/2 c. whipping cream, whipped
6 c. hot milk

Melt chocolate in a double boiler over medium heat. Add water; stir constantly for 4 minutes. Add sugar and salt; cook 4 minutes longer, stirring constantly. Cool mixture; fold in whipped cream. To serve, place a heaping tablespoon of chocolate mixture into each serving cup and pour about one cup hot milk on top, or until cup is almost filled. Stir lightly to blend. Serves 8.

Tag sales and flea markets are the best places to find tea cups, mugs and even kid-size cups. Mixing and matching colors and patterns for serving tea, cocoa or punch is half the fun!

FAVORITE FALL
Sippers

Bewitching Brew

Brenda Huey
Geneva, IN

So tasty for little ghosts and goblins to enjoy after trick-or-treating!

14-oz. can sweetened
   condensed milk
46-oz. can pineapple juice,
   chilled

2 ltrs. orange soda, chilled
Garnish: orange sherbet

Combine condensed milk, pineapple juice and orange soda in a punch bowl. Top with scoops of orange sherbet, as desired. Makes 4 quarts.

Kids will giggle over the floating "hands"
in their Bewitching Brew! Rinse out a pair of vinyl gloves
and fill with water. Tie the ends tightly into knots
and place in the freezer. When frozen, cut off the knots,
remove the gloves and place in punch.

Russian Tea Mix

Teresa Stiegelmeyer
Indianapolis, IN

Keep this mix in the pantry for a quick & easy fall sipper.

1/2 c. orange drink mix
1/3 c. unsweetened
   instant tea mix
1/4 c. sugar

3 T. lemonade drink mix
1/4 t. cinnamon
1/8 t. ground cloves

Combine all ingredients and store in an airtight container. Use one to 2 teaspoons of tea mix per cup of boiling water. Makes about one cup.

Frosty Fall Punch

Kelly Alderson
Erie, PA

A refreshing twist on punch...everyone will love it!

1 c. sugar
1 c. strong brewed tea
4 c. orange juice

4 c. pineapple juice
4 c. lemonade
2 ltrs. ginger ale, chilled

Combine sugar and tea in a pitcher; stir until sugar is dissolved. Stir in orange juice, pineapple juice and lemonade; chill 4 hours. Just before serving, pour chilled juice mixture into a punch bowl and stir in ginger ale. Makes 24 servings.

Spoon Russian Tea Mix into old-fashioned canning jars and tie on handmade tags for sharing with friends. Tuck inside a basket alongside apples, mini pumpkins, Indian corn and gourds...what fall fun!

Citrus Slush

Aryn Lentz
Camp Hill, PA

There's nothing else I can say...this is great!

9 c. water
4 c. sugar
12-oz. can frozen lemonade
  concentrate, thawed

12-oz. can frozen orange juice
  concentrate, thawed
3 to 4 ltrs. lemon-lime soda,
  chilled

Bring water and sugar to a boil in a medium saucepan over medium-high heat. Reduce heat; simmer for 15 minutes until sugar is dissolved. Stir in lemonade and orange juice; let cool for 30 minutes. Pour into a large container and freeze overnight, or to desired consistency. To serve, pour about 3/4 cup soda in a tall glass. Add one scoop slush. Serves 50 to 60.

Fall means back-to-school, so whip up some tasty treats and greet the kids at the door. Spread out a quilt under the maple tree and spend some quiet time together hearing all about their day.

Amaretto Tea

Judy Taylor
Butler, MO

The almond extract gives this tea a tasty twist.

8-1/2 c. water, divided
1 family-size teabag
12-oz. can frozen lemonade
   concentrate

1 T. almond extract
1 to 1-1/2 c. sugar

Bring 4 cups water to a rolling boil; pour over teabag. Steep for 3 to 5 minutes; discard teabag and set aside. In a 2-quart pitcher, mix together frozen lemonade and remaining water. Add brewed tea, almond extract and enough water to fill the pitcher. Add at least one cup sugar, stirring frequently before serving. Serves 6 to 8.

Invite girlfriends over for afternoon tea...a relaxing way for friends to catch up. Have on hand yummy scones, cinnamon toast and marmalade along with finger sandwiches. Set out plenty of honey, lemon slices, sugar cubes and half-and-half so everyone can have their tea just the way they like it.

Old-Fashioned Hot Chocolate

Dana Iungerich
Frisco, TX

Hmmm, what could be better than 4 kinds of chocolate?

1/3 c. sugar
1/4 c. baking cocoa
1/4 t. salt
3 c. milk, divided
3/4 t. vanilla extract
1 c. whipping cream

1-oz. sq. bittersweet baking
   chocolate
1-oz. sq. white melting chocolate
3/4 c. whipping cream, whipped
6 t. mini semi-sweet chocolate
   chips

Combine sugar, cocoa, salt and 1/2 cup milk in a medium bowl; beat until smooth. Pour into a slow cooker; add remaining milk and vanilla. Cover and cook on low setting for 2 hours. Add cream; cover and cook on low setting for an additional 10 minutes. Stir in baking and melting chocolates until smooth. Divide hot chocolate into 6 mugs; top each with 2 tablespoons whipped cream and one teaspoon mini chocolate chips. Serves 6.

The prettiest pumpkins! Spread white glue over a small pumpkin and place it on sheets of newspaper. Sprinkle powder glitter over the glue, completely covering the pumpkin. Let dry for one hour, then shake off any excess glitter.

Fruity Spiced Tea

Lynda Robson
Boston, MA

A delicious blend of fruit juices and spices.

6 c. boiling water
1 T. unsweetened
   instant tea mix
1/2 t. allspice
1/2 t. cinnamon
1/2 t. nutmeg

3-oz. pkg. cherry gelatin mix
1 c. orange juice
1/4 c. lemon juice
4 c. cranberry juice cocktail
1/2 c. sugar

Pour boiling water into a heat-safe pitcher. Place tea and spices in cheesecloth; steep in boiling water for 5 minutes. Remove and discard cheesecloth; stir in gelatin and let cool. Add juices and sugar; stir until sugar is dissolved. Serve warm. Refrigerate any extra. Makes 3 quarts.

My kitchen linoleum is so black and shiny
that I waltz while I wait for the kettle to boil.

-Florida Scott-Maxwell

FAVORITE FALL
Sippers

Sweater Weather Tea

Robin Hill
Rochester, NY

Play outside, then come in and warm up to a mug of tea!

6 c. water
3/4 c. sugar
1 c. unsweetened instant
    tea mix

8 whole cloves
2 4-inch cinnamon sticks
2-1/2 c. red fruit punch
1/4 c. lemon juice

Combine water, sugar, instant tea mix, cloves and cinnamon sticks in a large saucepan. Bring to a boil over high heat, stirring occasionally. Boil for 2 to 4 minutes; remove whole spices, if desired. Stir in fruit punch and lemon juice; warm through. Serve hot. Makes 8 servings.

Not too hot, not too cold...autumn is a great time for getting outside. Place a hook by the back door and keep a favorite sweater on it. You never know when you'll want to run outside to see the colorful trees or a harvest moon.

Apple Dapple Punch

Connie Bryant
Topeka, KS

Great for any fall celebration or family get-together.

32-oz. bottle apple juice, chilled
12-oz. can frozen cranberry
  juice cocktail concentrate,
  thawed

1 c. orange juice
1-1/2 ltrs. ginger ale, chilled
Garnish: apple slices

Combine apple juice, cranberry juice concentrate and orange juice in a large punch bowl; stir until dissolved. Slowly pour in ginger ale. Float apple slices on top of punch. Makes 12 servings.

Create a warm glow using box graters picked up at flea markets. The more character, the better, so look for ones that have darkened with age and are even a bit worn. Pick up a variety of sizes and simply tuck a votive or tealight inside. So simple!

Favorite Fall Sippers

Cranberry Slush

Judy Borecky
Escondido, CA

Create a festive garnish...just slip the cranberries and orange slices on a wooden skewer.

3/4 c. sugar
8 c. water, divided
12-oz. can frozen orange juice
    concentrate
12-oz. can frozen cranberry
    juice cocktail concentrate

6-oz. can frozen limeade
    concentrate
2 c. white grape juice
2 ltrs. lemon-lime soda, chilled
Optional: fresh cranberries,
    orange slices

In a large saucepan over medium heat, dissolve sugar in 2 cups water. Add next 4 ingredients and remaining water. Pour into a freezer-safe container; freeze until solid. To serve, place 2 scoops slush mixture into glasses. Pour lemon-lime soda over top until nearly full. Garnish with fresh cranberries and orange slices, if desired. Serves 30 to 40.

For the best of the bounty, head to the pumpkin patch early! Just fill a wheelbarrow with pumpkins, squash and gourds for an oh-so-simple harvest decoration. Add some fun with white Lumina pumpkins or orange-red Cinderella pumpkins.

Mexican Hot Chocolate

Flo Burtnett
Gage, OK

*Serve up this scrumptious hot cocoa...it has a hint of
cinnamon and vanilla flavors.*

1/2 c. sugar
1/2 c. baking cocoa
3/4 t. cinnamon

6 c. milk
2 t. vanilla extract

Combine sugar, cocoa and cinnamon in a small saucepan; gradually stir in milk. Warm over medium heat, stirring constantly, until hot without bringing to a boil. Remove from heat; stir in vanilla. Serves 6.

Leaf peeping is just a fun way of enjoying all the russet reds
and golds that can be found as the leaves change colors.
Get together with your best friends and leaf peep while
tag sale-ing or checking out the local pumpkin patch
and farmers' market!

Minty Hot Cocoa

Angela Wilder
Georgetown, KY

Mint patties are the secret to this sweet treat.

3 c. milk, divided
8 small chocolate-covered mint
   patties, chopped

1/8 t. salt
1 c. whipping cream

Combine 1/2 cup milk with peppermint patties in a saucepan over medium-low heat until patties are melted. Stir until smooth; add salt and remaining milk. Bring to a simmer; stir in cream. Serve immediately. Serves 6.

There is no doubt that running away on a fresh
blue morning can be exhilarating.

-Jean Rhys

Razzleberry Tea

Susan deGraaff
Nicholasville, KY

*Sweet raspberries combine with tangy lemonade
to make a fruity warm tea.*

8 c. water, divided
5 teabags
1-1/4 c. sugar
6-oz. can frozen lemonade
   concentrate, thawed

64-oz. bottle cranberry-
   raspberry juice, chilled
10-oz. pkg. frozen raspberries,
   thawed

Bring 3 cups water to a boil in a saucepan. Remove from heat;
add teabags and let steep until tea is desired strength. Discard
teabags. While still warm, stir in sugar until dissolved; add enough
of remaining water to equal 2 quarts total. Pour tea into a large
serving pitcher. Stir in remaining ingredients; serve warm or chilled.
Makes 24 servings.

Head out to the apple orchard for a day of fun.
The kids will love it, and you'll come home with bushels
of the best-tasting apples for crisps, pies and cobblers!

FARM-FRESH
Breakfasts

Fall Harvest French Toast

Roxanne Anderson
Williams, IA

My family loves this dish for brunch on a cool fall day. I've even mixed it up the night before and refrigerated for an easy and delicious overnight casserole. Just bake 10 minutes longer than directed below.

12 slices Texas toast, crusts
   trimmed
6 eggs, beaten
1 c. milk
3 tart apples, cored, peeled and
   chopped
3/4 c. chopped walnuts

3 T. butter
1/3 c. maple syrup
2 t. cinnamon
1/2 c. sweetened, dried
   cranberries
Garnish: powdered sugar,
   additional maple syrup

Cube bread and place in a lightly greased 13"x9" baking pan; set aside. Place eggs in a medium bowl; set aside. Pour milk into a microwave-safe container; microwave on high setting until hot, 1-1/2 to 2 minutes. Whisk milk into eggs, stirring constantly; pour over bread cubes and set aside. Combine apples, walnuts, butter, syrup and cinnamon in a skillet over medium heat; cook until apples are slightly tender. Pour apple mixture over bread cubes; sprinkle with cranberries. Press down lightly to make sure bread is well soaked. Bake at 375 degrees for 30 to 35 minutes, or until set in center. Sprinkle with powdered sugar; serve with maple syrup. Makes 6 servings.

Set pillar candles in a canning jar that's partially filled with candy corn, orange and yellow jelly beans or acorns...sets a fall mood instantly for any breakfast table!

Pumpkin Pancakes

Diana Schumacher
Springfield, IL

I enjoy making these tasty pancakes with the pumpkins that my husband, Dan, grows every year in our backyard.

1 c. all-purpose flour
2 T. dark brown sugar, packed
2 t. baking powder
1 t. pumpkin pie spice
1 c. milk

1 c. pumpkin, cooked and
  mashed
2 eggs, separated
1/3 c. oil
Garnish: maple syrup

Combine first 4 ingredients in a large mixing bowl; stir well and set aside. Combine milk, pumpkin and egg yolks; add to dry ingredients, stirring until smooth. Using an electric mixer at high speed, beat egg whites until stiff peaks form; gently fold into pumpkin mixture. Heat oil on a non-stick griddle over medium heat; ladle about 1/3 cup batter onto griddle. Turn pancakes when tops are covered with bubbles and edges look done; cook until golden on other side. Serve with maple syrup. Makes 12 to 14 pancakes.

Why not have a crackling fire in the fireplace while everyone's enjoying breakfast? What a toasty way to warm up the family on a chilly morning!

Chocolatey Gingerbread Waffles   *Vickie*

So yummy!

1 c. molasses
1/2 c. butter
1-1/2 t. baking soda
1/2 c. milk
1 egg, beaten

2 c. all-purpose flour
1-1/2 t. ground ginger
1/2 t. cinnamon
1/2 t. salt

Combine molasses and butter in a small saucepan; cook over medium heat until almost boiling. Remove from heat and let cool slightly. Stir in baking soda, milk and egg; set aside. Stir together flour, spices and salt in a mixing bowl. Make a well in the center and pour in molasses mixture; stir until smooth. Pour about 1/2 cup batter onto preheated waffle iron sprayed with non-stick vegetable spray; bake as manufacturer directs. Serve hot; drizzle with Hot Chocolate Sauce. Makes about 6 waffles.

Hot Chocolate Sauce:

2 c. water
1 c. sugar
1/2 c. baking cocoa
2 T. cornstarch

1 t. salt
2 t. vanilla extract
2 T. butter

Put water in a small saucepan; bring to a boil. Add sugar, cocoa, cornstarch and salt. Cook over medium heat, stirring constantly, until mixture comes to a boil. Remove from heat; add vanilla and butter. Stir until smooth.

Maple-Sausage Breakfast Casserole
Denise Trigo
Downingtown, PA

When I make and take this to the office, I always prepare a side dish for my husband...he loves it!

1 lb. ground pork sausage
1/4 c. maple syrup
1/4 c. margarine, melted
7 slices country potato bread, torn

8-oz. pkg. shredded Cheddar cheese
5 eggs
1 pt. half-and-half
1 t. salt

Brown sausage in a skillet over medium heat; drain. Reduce heat and stir in syrup; remove from heat. Spread margarine in a 13"x9" baking pan; arrange bread over margarine. Spoon sausage mixture over bread; sprinkle with cheese. Blend together eggs, half-and-half and salt; pour over cheese. Cover and chill for 8 hours to overnight. Uncover and bake at 350 degrees for 40 to 50 minutes. Serves 6 to 8.

A centerpiece in a snap! Set a plump pumpkin in the center of the table and surround with bittersweet vines and tiny Baby Boo or Jack-be-Little pumpkins.

Cheesy Bacon Casserole

Laura Strausberger
Roswell, GA

Just the right size casserole for a small family.
Double the recipe if you want to feed more.

4 slices white bread, crusts
    trimmed
4 eggs, beaten
1-1/2 c. milk
1 t. dry mustard

1/2 t. dried, chopped onion
8 slices bacon, crisply cooked
    and crumbled
1 c. shredded Cheddar cheese

Arrange bread slices in a lightly greased 8"x8" baking pan; set aside.
Stir together eggs, milk, mustard and onion; pour over bread. Sprinkle
with bacon; cover and refrigerate 8 hours or overnight. Let stand at
room temperature for 30 minutes; uncover and bake at 350 degrees
for 20 minutes. Sprinkle with cheese and bake an additional
5 minutes, until cheese melts. Makes 4 servings.

Dress up breakfast cups and napkins!
Press leaf and pumpkin stickers on plain paper cups,
and use rubber stamps on paper napkins.

Farmhouse Favorite Sausage

Ginny Clarke
Independence, MO

An old-fashioned breakfast dish sure to stick to your ribs!

2 lbs. ground pork sausage
7-1/2 c. water, divided
1-1/2 t. salt

3/4 t. dried sage
1-1/2 c. yellow cornmeal
2 to 3 T. oil

Break up sausage in a medium saucepan; add 6 cups water. Heat to boiling; reduce heat and simmer for 20 minutes. Drain sausage, reserving 4-1/2 cups broth. Return sausage and reserved broth to pan; add salt and sage. Bring to a boil. In a mixing bowl, combine cornmeal with remaining water; gradually stir into sausage mixture. Cover and cook over low heat for 10 minutes, stirring occasionally. Pour into 2 ungreased 9"x5" loaf pans; cool and chill overnight. Remove from pans and slice 1/4 to 1/2-inch thick. Heat oil in a skillet over medium heat and fry until golden. Serves 8 to 10.

Whip up some birdseed bagels so the birds can enjoy breakfast as the season turns chilly. Just spread peanut butter on the cut side of a bagel; coat with birdseed. Slip a length of raffia in the bagel hole and hang from a tree. Be sure to continue feeding the birds throughout the fall and winter...they'll become dependent on the seeds, nuts and water you provide.

Nutty Pecan Popovers

Debbie Byrne
Clinton, CT

Delicious! Deliver a basket to your neighbors on a frosty morn.

4 eggs
2 c. milk
3 T. butter, melted

2 c. all-purpose flour
1/2 t. salt
1/3 c. pecans, finely chopped

Whisk together eggs, milk and butter in a large bowl. Add flour and salt, stirring until smooth. Stir in pecans. Spoon into 12 greased 6-ounce custard cups, filling 1/2 full. Arrange cups on a baking sheet. Bake at 400 degrees for 40 minutes, or until firm. Immediately pierce popovers with a fork to release steam. Serve hot with Honey Butter. Makes one dozen.

Honey Butter:

1/2 c. butter, softened

2 T. honey

Stir butter and honey together in a small bowl. Chill until serving time.

Slip a dress and apron on your scarecrow this season and she'll be an instant hit as a scarecrone!

Apple & Raisin Oatmeal

Debra Brooke
Branson, MO

Oatmeal with a hint of maple flavor.

2 c. water
1/4 t. cinnamon
1 c. quick-cooking oats,
   uncooked
3/4 c. apple, cored, peeled and
   finely chopped

1/3 c. raisins
2 T. maple syrup, divided
1/2 to 3/4 c. milk
brown sugar to taste

Combine water and cinnamon in a saucepan; bring to a boil over medium heat. Add oats; cook and stir for 3 minutes. Reduce heat to low; stir in apple, raisins and one tablespoon maple syrup. Cook for an additional 5 minutes. Add milk and sugar to taste; drizzle with remaining maple syrup. Serves 2.

Looking for a clever cooler? Breakfast will be oh-so fun with bottles of juice and milk tucked into a pumpkin-turned-ice bucket! Cut the top third off of a large pumpkin and clean out the inside. Line the pumpkin with a plastic bowl, fill with ice and juice bottles or boxes.

Savory Breakfast Pancakes

Jessica Parker
Mulvane, KS

Give the kids the unexpected for breakfast...these will disappear fast!

2 c. biscuit baking mix
1 c. milk
2 eggs
1/2 c. shredded mozzarella
　cheese
1/2 c. pepperoni, chopped

1/2 c. tomato, chopped
1/4 c. green pepper, chopped
2 t. Italian seasoning
Garnish: pizza sauce, grated
　Parmesan cheese

Stir together baking mix, milk and eggs until well blended; add cheese, pepperoni, tomato, green pepper and Italian seasoning. Heat a lightly greased griddle over medium-high heat. Ladle 1/4 cup batter onto the griddle; cook until golden on both sides. Garnish with pizza sauce and Parmesan cheese. Makes 15 pancakes.

If you were to ask me what is most important in a home,
I would say memories.

-Lillian Gish

Grandmommy's Casserole

Stephanie Onick
El Paso, TX

As a child, Grandmommy always let me help her make this dish and have a cup of coffee with her, which was such a treat.

1 lb. ground pork sausage,
   browned and drained
6 slices bread, torn
4-oz. can chopped green chiles
8-oz. pkg. shredded Cheddar
   cheese

6 eggs
1 c. milk
salt and pepper to taste

Mix together sausage, bread, chiles and cheese in a large bowl; set aside. Blend together eggs, milk, salt and pepper; stir into sausage mixture. Pour into a greased 13"x9" baking pan; cover and refrigerate overnight. Uncover and bake at 350 degrees for 50 minutes. Makes 6 to 8 servings.

When family & friends arrive for a visit, make the guest room comfy. Add a cozy quilt to the bed along with some feather pillows and toasty flannel sheets. Set out a few of your favorite books and fill a hollowed-out pumpkin with fresh mums. So pretty!

Sugary Cinnamon Roll-Ups

Vicki Norman
Corydon, KY

So yummy alongside a glass of frosty milk.

1 c. sugar
1 T. cinnamon
1 loaf sliced white bread
8-oz. pkg. cream cheese,
    softened

1 egg white
1/2 c. powdered sugar
1/2 c. butter, melted

Mix sugar and cinnamon in a small bowl; set aside. Using a rolling pin, roll bread slices to 1/4-inch thick. Blend together cream cheese, egg white and powdered sugar until smooth. Spread mixture evenly on one side of each bread slice; roll up. Roll each in melted butter, then in sugar mixture. Arrange roll-ups on a baking sheet lightly sprayed with non-stick vegetable spray. Bake at 350 degrees for 15 to 20 minutes. Makes about 14 to 20.

Top slices of toast or even pancakes and waffles with yummy Blueberry-Honey Butter. You can even serve it out of a hollowed-out Baby Boo pumpkin! In a food processor, blend one pound unsalted butter, slightly softened, with one pint ripe blueberries and 1/4 cup honey until smooth.

Best-Ever Sticky Buns

Jodi Schlichting
Cherokee, IA

To save time in the morning, these can be prepared the night before.

3-1/4 c. all-purpose flour,
   divided
2 envs. active dry yeast
3/4 c. milk
1/2 c. water

1/4 c. margarine, softened
1/4 c. sugar
1 t. salt
1 egg

Stir together 1-1/2 cups flour and yeast in a large bowl; set aside.
Combine milk, water, margarine, sugar and salt in a saucepan. Heat
until warm, about 120 to 130 degrees; add to flour mixture. Add egg;
beat with an electric mixer on high speed for 3 minutes. Stir in
remaining flour by hand; cover and let rise for 30 minutes. Pour hot
topping into a lightly greased 13"x9" baking pan. Punch down dough
and drop onto topping by tablespoonfuls. Bake at 375 degrees for
20 minutes, or until golden. Let cool for one minute; invert onto a
serving tray. Makes one dozen.

Topping:

3/4 c. margarine
1 c. brown sugar, packed
2 t. cinnamon

1 T. light corn syrup
1 T. water

Combine ingredients in a microwave-safe container. Microwave on
high setting until brown sugar dissolves, about 3 minutes, stirring
once every minute.

Reuben Brunch Bake

Debi DeVore
Dover, OH

All the flavor of a Reuben sandwich in a savory breakfast bake!

8 eggs, beaten
14-1/2 oz. can sauerkraut,
   drained and rinsed
8-oz. pkg. shredded
   Swiss cheese
2-1/2 oz. pkg. deli corned beef,
   cut into 1/2-inch pieces
1/2 c. green onion, chopped

1/2 c. milk
1 T. Dijon mustard
1/4 t. salt
1/4 t. pepper
3 slices rye bread, toasted
   and torn
1/4 c. butter, melted

Combine all ingredients except bread and butter, in a large bowl; pour into a greased 11"x7" baking pan. Cover and refrigerate overnight. Remove from refrigerator; let stand 30 minutes. Toss toasted rye bread with melted butter; sprinkle over casserole. Bake, uncovered, at 350 degrees for 40 to 45 minutes, or until a knife inserted near the middle comes out clean. Let stand 10 minutes before serving. Serves 8 to 12.

Protect favorite recipes on laminated cards that are easy to wipe clean. Easy-to-use laminating sheets can be found at any office supply store. Place the recipe on the bottom laminating sheet and carefully lay the top sheet over the recipe cards, smoothing out any wrinkles.

Texas-Style Breakfast Casserole

Cynde Sonnier
La Porte, TX

I hosted an old-fashioned pancake supper for my husband's 40th birthday, and thinking the ladies might like something other than pancakes, I prepared this casserole. Well, the men left the pancakes for this dish and even asked for seconds!

32-oz. pkg. frozen shredded
    hashbrowns
1 lb. cooked ham, diced
1-1/2 c. shredded
    Cheddar cheese
Optional: 2 pickled jalapeños,
    chopped

8 eggs
1 c. whipping cream
1/2 t. garlic powder
1/8 t. nutmeg
salt and pepper to taste
1 bunch green onions, sliced

Place frozen hashbrowns in the bottom of a 13"x9" baking pan sprayed with non-stick vegetable spray. Top with ham, cheese and jalapeños, if using; set aside. In a large bowl, combine eggs, cream and seasonings; mix well. Pour egg mixture over casserole; top with onions. Bake at 350 degrees for 55 minutes. Makes 8 to 10 servings.

Surprise a friend or neighbor with a homemade muffin or scone...in a trick-or-treat bag! It's so simple. Just place the muffin in an orange paper bag and gather together the top of the bag; secure with a rubber band. Hide the rubber band with green florists' tape. What fun!

Omelets in a Bag

Patricia Wulff
Sedgwick, KS

A fun breakfast idea that really works! I like to serve them with fresh fruit and coffee cake on the side.

2 eggs
cooked sausage
chopped ham
shredded cheeses
chopped onion

chopped green pepper
chopped tomato
chopped mushrooms
salsa

Have each guest write his or her name with permanent pen on a quart-size plastic zipping freezer bag. Place 2 eggs in bag and shake to scramble. Add other ingredients to bag as desired. Press the air out of bag and zip it up. Bring a large pot of water to a rolling boil; place 6 to 8 bags at a time into pot. Boil bags for 13 to 15 minutes. When done, open bags and omelets will roll out easily. Make as many as needed.

Who says you have to carve a pumpkin? Kids will giggle when they see your mop-top lion! Color a new mop head with fabric dye, saving a few strands for his eyebrows. Just use tacky glue to hold them in place. Acrylic paint is ideal for creating his eyes, nose and mouth.

Crispy Home Fries

Carol Kuhns
Gooseberry Patch

*There's nothing like golden home fries paired with eggs,
bacon, toast and juice for breakfast.*

2 lbs. Yukon Gold potatoes,
   peeled and cubed
2 lbs. sweet potatoes,
   peeled and cubed
3 T. butter

1 onion, coarsely chopped
2 cloves garlic, finely chopped
3/4 t. salt
1/2 t. pepper

Place Yukon Gold potatoes in a large saucepan; cover with water.
Bring to a boil over high heat; boil for 2 minutes. Add sweet potatoes
and return to a boil. Cook for 10 to 12 minutes, until potatoes are
tender. Drain; let cool on a baking sheet. Melt butter over medium
heat in a large skillet. Add onion and sauté 5 to 7 minutes, until
softened. Add garlic; sauté an additional minute. Add potatoes, salt
and pepper to skillet. Cook, stirring occasionally, until golden and
tender, 15 to 20 minutes. Makes 8 servings.

Warm up a chilly morning with a mug of chocolatey cocoa.
Make it extra special by topping it off with a dollop of
sweetened whipped cream. Beat together 1/2 pint whipping
cream with one tablespoon sugar and one teaspoon vanilla
until soft peaks form. So yummy!

Apple Scones

Jennifer Best
Phelan, CA

A favorite of mine from an old 1950's cookbook. I've even prepared it with dried cherries in place of apples...my kids love them!

2 c. all-purpose flour
1 t. baking powder
1 t. salt
3 T. butter
1/4 c. sugar

1 c. apple, cored, peeled
  and minced
1 egg, beaten
2/3 c. milk
Garnish: 2 T. butter, 2 T. sugar

Stir together flour, baking powder and salt in a mixing bowl. Cut in butter; add sugar and apple. Mix in egg and milk; stir until a soft dough forms. Knead until well blended. Spread in a greased 12"x8" baking pan. Bake for 25 minutes at 450 degrees. Cut into 2"x2" squares; cut each square in half diagonally. Spread tops with butter; sprinkle generously with sugar. Serve warm. Makes 4 dozen.

Devonshire Cream

Jackie Crough
Salina, KS

If you have not tasted a scone with jam and Devonshire Cream, you have missed out on one of the greatest tastes!

1 t. unflavored gelatin
3/4 c. cold water
1 c. whipping cream

1/2 c. sugar
1-1/2 t. vanilla extract
8-oz. container sour cream

Combine gelatin and water in a small saucepan; heat until gelatin dissolves. Let cool and set aside. Place cream, sugar and vanilla in a mixing bowl; beat with an electric mixer on high speed until soft peaks form. Stir sour cream into gelatin; fold gelatin mixture into whipped cream. Store in refrigerator in an airtight container. Makes 3 cups.

Farm-Fresh Breakfasts

Gingerbread Pancakes

Charmie Fisher
Fontana, CA

These have a wonderful taste...good with Lemon Sauce, or even just sprinkled with powdered sugar and served with syrup.

1-1/2 c. all-purpose flour
1 t. baking powder
1/4 t. baking soda
1 t. cinnamon
1/2 t. ground ginger

1/4 t. salt
1 egg
1-1/4 c. milk
1/4 c. molasses
3 T. oil

Stir together flour, baking powder, baking soda, spices and salt in a small bowl; set aside. Beat together egg and milk in a large bowl; stir in molasses, then oil. Add flour mixture; stir just until combined. Lightly grease a griddle or skillet; heat until a drop of water dances on it. Pour 1/4 cup batter onto griddle; cook until puffed and bubbly. Turn; cook until other side is golden. Serve with Lemon Sauce. Makes 12.

Lemon Sauce:

1/2 c. sugar
1 T. cornstarch
1 c. hot water

2 T. butter
2 T. lemon juice

Combine sugar and cornstarch in a medium saucepan; gradually mix in water. Cook and stir over medium heat until mixture is thick and clear. Add butter and lemon juice; stir until butter melts. Keep warm.

There is music in the meadows, in the air...autumn is here.

-William Stanley Braithwaite

Herbed Quiche

Jennifer Niemi
Nova Scotia, Canada

This recipe is quick & easy, and so good, I just had to share it!

1/4 c. butter
1 c. onion, finely chopped
1 T. all-purpose flour
1-1/4 c. milk, divided
4 eggs
1/8 t. salt

1/8 t. pepper
3 T. fresh parsley, finely chopped
1 T. fresh chives, finely chopped
1 c. Swiss cheese, diced
9-inch deep-dish pie crust

In a heavy skillet, melt butter over medium heat. Add onion; cook until softened. Stir in flour and 1/2 cup milk, mixing well. Cook until thickened, stirring constantly. Remove from heat and set aside. Beat together eggs, remaining milk, salt and pepper. Add herbs and cheese; mix well. Place pie crust into pie plate; flute edges. Stir onion mixture into egg mixture; pour into unbaked pie crust. Bake at 425 degrees for 15 minutes; reduce heat to 350 degrees and bake an additional 25 to 35 minutes, or until a knife inserted near the center comes out clean. Cut into wedges. Makes 6 servings.

Carve your house number into the front of a Jack-'O-Lantern, set on the front steps and slip a lighted votive inside. What a fun way to help guests find their way to your home!

Bacon & Egg Filled Tomatoes

Wendy Jacobs
Idaho Falls, SD

Not only so tasty, it's pretty enough to serve overnight guests.

4 tomatoes, tops removed
6 eggs, beaten
1/2 t. Dijon mustard
4 green onions, thinly sliced
2 T. fresh basil, chopped
salt and pepper to taste

8 slices bacon, crisply cooked
    and crumbled
1/4 c. butter, melted
1/2 c. shredded Monterey
    Jack cheese

Scoop out insides of tomatoes, leaving a thick shell. Invert tomatoes on a paper towel to drain for 15 minutes. Whisk together eggs, mustard, onions, basil, salt and pepper in a bowl. Stir in bacon; set aside. Arrange tomatoes in an 8"x8" baking pan sprayed with non-stick vegetable spray; bake at 400 degrees for 5 minutes. Pour one tablespoon melted butter into each tomato; divide egg mixture among tomatoes. Top with cheese. Return to oven; bake for an additional 10 minutes, or just until eggs are set. Serves 4.

When frying bacon, here's the best way to drain it. Place the cooked bacon slices on top of the spatter screen and place it over a bowl. The drippings will go through the screen and into the bowl...so easy!

Country Breakfast Sandwiches

Jo Ann

Why not try pancakes or toasted bagels in place of the toast for a change? So scrumptious!

3 T. butter, divided
1 Granny Smith apple, peeled,
   cored and thinly sliced
2 slices whole-wheat bread,
   toasted

3 links pork sausage, halved
   lengthwise and browned
1/4 c. maple syrup, warmed

Heat 2 tablespoons butter in a skillet over low heat. Add apple; sauté until tender and golden, turning often. Spread toasted bread with remaining butter; top each slice with sausages, apple slices and syrup. Makes 2 servings.

Some of the days in November carry the whole memory of summer as a fire opal carries the color of moonrise.

-Gladys Taber

Apple-Waffle Sandwiches

Jackie Smulski
Lyons, IL

Pair this up with fresh sliced fruit to round out
a wonderful breakfast or brunch.

3 T. butter, divided
8 frozen waffles, thawed
8 slices American cheese

2 Granny Smith apples, cored,
  peeled and very thinly sliced

Melt 1-1/2 tablespoons butter in a large skillet over medium heat; add 2 waffles. Top each with one cheese slice, one-quarter of apple slices and another cheese slice; top each with another waffle. Cook until waffles are lightly toasted on both sides and cheese is melted. Repeat with remaining ingredients; serve immediately. Makes 4 servings.

Invite neighbors over for a fall breakfast...outside around the fire ring or inside by the fireplace. It's a great way to catch up with one another.

Fruit & Nut Bread

Karen Pilcher
Burleson, TX

An unusual ingredient combination, but absolutely the best bread.

1-3/4 c. all-purpose flour
1/2 c. sugar
2 t. baking powder
1/2 t. baking soda
1/4 t. salt
2 eggs
1/2 c. butter, melted and cooled

8-oz. pkg. farmer's cheese or
   Muenster cheese, diced
3/4 c. milk
1 t. vanilla extract
1/2 lb. mixed dried, diced fruit
1 c. chopped walnuts or pecans

Mix together flour, sugar, baking powder, baking soda and salt in a large bowl; set aside. Whisk eggs into butter in a medium bowl; add remaining ingredients. Sprinkle flour mixture over egg mixture; stir until well blended. Spread in a greased 9" round springform pan. Bake at 350 degrees for 1-1/4 hours, until golden and a toothpick inserted in the center comes out clean. Serves 6 to 8.

Try steaming eggnog, instead of milk, for
cappuccino...sprinkle with pumpkin pie spice for a
warm-you-to-your-toes breakfast treat!

Autumn Pancakes

Kathy Grashoff
Fort Wayne, IN

Apples and walnuts just naturally go together!

1/2 c. quick-cooking oats,
  uncooked
1-1/2 c. boiling water
1-1/2 c. all-purpose flour
2 t. baking powder
1/8 t. salt
3 T. sugar
1/2 t. cinnamon

1 egg, beaten
1 c. milk
1 apple, cored, peeled and
  coarsely chopped
1/4 c. chopped walnuts
3 T. butter, melted
Garnish: maple syrup or
  powdered sugar

Place oats in a small bowl. Pour boiling water over oats and let stand 5 minutes; set aside. Combine flour, baking powder, salt, sugar and cinnamon in a large bowl. Add oat mixture, egg, milk, apple, nuts and melted butter; mix well. Pour batter by 1/4 cupfuls into a lightly greased skillet over medium-high heat. Cook until bubbles appear on the surface, about 2 minutes. Turn pancakes over and cook until golden, about one minute longer. Garnish with syrup or powdered sugar. Serves 6.

Serve Autumn Pancakes with cheery pumpkin faces! Cut an apple into thin slices, then cut triangles for the eyes and nose. Give Jack a happy smile with an apple slice for his mouth. Don't forget to dip the apple slices in lemon juice to keep them from browning.

Rise & Shine Quiche

Wendy Lee Paffenroth
Pine Island, NY

Biscuit baking mix makes this tasty breakfast dish a snap to prepare.

1/2 lb. bacon
1 onion, chopped
8 eggs
2-1/4 c. milk
1/2 c. shredded Swiss cheese

1-1/2 c. biscuit baking mix
1/4 c. fresh parsley, snipped
salt and pepper to taste
Garnish: paprika

Crisply cook bacon in a skillet over medium heat; crumble and set aside. Drain, reserving one tablespoon drippings. Sauté onion in drippings until tender, about 2 to 3 minutes. Layer bacon and onion in a greased 13"x9" baking pan; set aside. Beat eggs in a large bowl; stir in milk. Add remaining ingredients, except paprika, and pour over bacon mixture; sprinkle with paprika. Bakc at 400 degrees for 15 minutes. Reduce heat to 350 degrees and bake an additional 30 minutes, until a knife inserted in the center comes out clean. Let stand about 10 minutes; cut into squares. Makes 12 servings.

Vintage-style postcards make terrific fall decorations. Tuck them between gourds and mini pumpkins on the mantel or make color copies and secure around a canning jar candle. Just tie on a tag for a clever hostess gift.

Country Morning Bacon Muffins

Tina Wright
Atlanta, GA

Good enough to coax you out of bed on a chilly morning!

2 c. all-purpose flour
1 T. baking powder
1/4 t. baking soda
2 T. sugar
1 T. wheat germ
1/2 t. salt
2 eggs, beaten

1/3 c. milk
1/4 c. butter, melted
1/4 c. oil
1 c. creamed corn
4 slices bacon, crisply cooked
    and crumbled

Combine flour, baking powder, baking soda, sugar, wheat germ and salt in a large mixing bowl; set aside. Stir together eggs, milk, butter and oil in a medium mixing bowl. Add corn and bacon; mix well. Stir egg mixture into flour mixture just until combined. Spoon into greased muffin cups, filling 2/3 full. Bake at 375 degrees for 20 to 25 minutes, until golden. Makes one dozen.

Serve fuss-free favorites like Country Morning
Bacon Muffins...ideal for overnight guests on Thanksgiving
morning. Everyone can easily help themselves while the
day's fun is beginning.

Mom's Instant Coffee Bars

Kim Malusky
Twinsburg, OH

*I used to love it when my mom would make these. I wasn't
old enough to drink coffee, so eating them made me feel "grown up."*

2 c. brown sugar, packed
1/2 c. butter, softened
2 eggs
3 c. all-purpose flour
1 t. salt
1 t. baking soda

1 t. cinnamon
1 t. instant coffee granules
1 c. boiling water
1/2 c. chopped nuts
12-oz. pkg. semi-sweet
    chocolate chips

Blend together brown sugar and butter in a large mixing bowl. Add
eggs; mix well. Add flour, salt, baking soda and cinnamon. Mix well;
set aside. Dissolve coffee in boiling water; stir into mixture. Fold in
nuts and chocolate chips. Spread in a baking sheet with bottom and
sides greased and floured. Bake at 350 degrees for 20 minutes.
Immediately frost with Coffee Frosting. Cut into squares. Makes
2 to 3 dozen.

Coffee Frosting:

1 c. powdered sugar
1 T. butter, softened

1 t. instant coffee granules
1 T. boiling water

Blend together powdered sugar and butter in a medium bowl; set
aside. Dissolve coffee in hot water; blend into sugar mixture.

When fall days are too
chilly to go outside, enjoy
some family fun inside!
Get out the crayons and
coloring books, make
your own paper dolls or
have a picnic in front of
the fireplace.

Hay-Day
Appetizers

Scrumptious Stuffed Potato Skins

Tammy Rowe
Fremont, OH

Scrumptious says it all! Easy to make and feeds a crowd.

4 baking potatoes, quartered
   lengthwise
olive oil
8-oz. container sour cream
1/3 c. shredded Cheddar cheese
1 t. garlic, minced

1 green onion, chopped
2 t. dried parsley
2 T. bacon bits
1/2 t. salt
1/2 t. pepper

Brush skins of potatoes with olive oil; arrange on a baking sheet cut-side up. Bake for 30 minutes at 400 degrees; let cool. Scoop out baked insides, leaving about 1/8-inch shells; reserve baked potato for another recipe. Mix together remaining ingredients; spoon into potato skins. Return to baking sheet; bake for an additional 20 minutes. Makes 16.

Host a fun-filled pumpkin carving party this year. Guests can bring their own pumpkins and tools, while you set out water-based paints, glue sticks, glitter and stickers for the kids.

HAY-DAY
Appetizers

Cheddar Cheese Ball

Mary Poole
St. Petersburg, FL

Serve surrounded with your favorite crackers.
For fun, roll them into mini cheese balls for easy nibbling.

1/4 lb. extra-sharp Cheddar
  cheese
1/3 c. butter
1/4 onion, chopped
1/2 t. regular or spicy mustard

1/2 t. prepared horseradish
1/2 t. garlic, minced
1/2 t. Worcestershire sauce
Garnish: chopped nuts or
  fresh parsley

Place cheese in a food processor; shred with shredding blade. Change
to chopping blade; add all remaining ingredients except garnish.
Process until mixture is blended and a small ball forms. Roll in nuts or
parsley. Wrap in plastic wrap and chill. Makes one cup.

Use tiered cake stands for bite-size appetizers...so handy,
and they take up less space on the buffet table than
setting out several serving platters.

Shoo Vampire Garlic Spread

David Wink
Gooseberry Patch

Not just for Halloween...a tasty hostess gift for any harvest get-together! Spoon into a crock and give with a basket of crackers.

8-oz. pkg. cream cheese,
   softened
1/2 c. butter, softened
3/4 t. dill weed
1/2 t. dried thyme

1/4 t. dried oregano
1/4 t. garlic powder
1/4 t. pepper
1/4 t. seasoned salt

Combine all ingredients in a food processor or mixer; blend well. Cover and chill for at least 2 hours, up to one week. Makes 1-1/2 cups.

Arrange tall veggies like carrots and celery
in bud vases or skinny hollowed-out
gourds...they'll add fun to any table!

HAY-DAY Appetizers

Oh-So-Cheesy Chili Dip

Suzy Grubich
Eighty Four, PA

Ready to enjoy in 7 minutes flat! Spoon into a white Baby Boo pumpkin surrounded by tortilla chips.

8-oz. pkg. cream cheese
15-oz. can chili

8-oz. pkg. shredded Cheddar cheese

Place cream cheese in a 9" glass pie plate; soften in microwave on high setting for one minute. Spread in pie plate. Spoon chili over cream cheese; top with shredded cheese. Microwave on high setting for 4 to 6 minutes, or until cheese is hot and bubbly. Serve warm. Makes about 4 cups.

Turn a cast-off dollhouse into a tabletop haunted mansion by painting it black. A ghostly greeting for family & friends!

Pumpkin Cheese Ball

Carol Hickman
Kingsport, TN

Such a cute (and yummy) cheese ball!

1/2 c. cream cheese, softened
   and divided
8-oz. pkg. shredded mild
   Cheddar cheese
1/4 c. canned pumpkin

1/4 c. pineapple preserves
1/4 t. allspice
1/4 t. nutmeg
1 pretzel rod, broken in half

Combine all ingredients except pretzel rod until well blended. Cover. Refrigerate for 2 to 3 hours; shape into a ball. Using a knife, score vertical lines down the sides. Insert pretzel rod half in center for stem. Makes 2 cups.

Ghostly Party Dip

Esther Dailey
Hesperia, CA

Disappears without a trace! Better double the recipe.

8-oz. pkg. cream cheese,
   softened
1/2 c. butter, softened
1 t. vanilla extract
3/4 c. powdered sugar

2 T. brown sugar, packed
3/4 c. mini semi-sweet
   chocolate chips
chocolate graham crackers

Combine cream cheese and butter in a large mixing bowl; mix well. Add remaining ingredients except crackers. Stir until completely mixed; chill until serving time. Serve with chocolate graham crackers. Makes 3 cups.

Autumn Harvest Fruit Dip

Kimberly Boyce
Murrieta, CA

Set out a variety of dippers for this treat
so everyone can choose their favorite.

8-oz. pkg. cream
   cheese, softened
3/4 c. brown sugar, packed
2 T. vanilla extract

2 t. maple extract
seedless red grapes, vanilla
   wafers, gingersnaps,
   graham cracker sticks

Combine first 4 ingredients in a mixing bowl. Blend with an electric
mixer on medium speed until smooth. Chill for at least one hour. Serve
with fruit and small cookies for dipping. Makes about 2 cups.

Cheesy Fruit & Nut Spread

Lisa Ashton
Aston, PA

Delicious spread on slices of nut bread too.

8-oz. pkg. cream cheese,
   softened
3 T. honey
1 T. apple brandy or apple juice
1/4 c. chopped pecans

1/2 c. dried, chopped
   apple pieces
apple and pear slices,
   assorted crackers

Mix together cream cheese, honey and brandy or juice until well
combined. Stir in pecans and apples. Cover and chill. Serve with fruit
slices and crackers for dipping. Makes about 2 cups.

Queso Blanco

Janice Woods
Northern Cambria, PA

*My daughter made this dip for her Spanish class and her
teacher said it was the best Queso Blanco she had ever tasted!*

1 c. finely shredded Monterey
   Jack cheese
4-oz. can diced green chiles
1/4 c. half-and-half
2 T. onion, finely chopped
2 t. ground cumin
1/2 t. salt

1/8 t. pepper
1 T. fresh cilantro,
   finely chopped
Optional: 1 serrano pepper,
   finely chopped
tortilla chips or flour tortillas

Combine all ingredients except tortillas in a double boiler. Cook over
medium heat until cheese is melted and well blended, stirring
occasionally. Serve with tortilla chips or hot flour tortillas.
Makes about 2 cups.

Fill windowboxes with mini pumpkins, gourds,
colorful leaves and bittersweet vines...a quick & easy
fall decoration that's finished in minutes.

Hot Bacon & Swiss Dip

Marla Caldwell
Forest, IN

Always a favorite...the flavor combination is unbeatable.

8-oz. pkg. cream cheese,
  softened
1/2 c. mayonnaise
1 c. shredded Swiss cheese
2 T. green onion, chopped

8 slices bacon, crisply cooked
  and crumbled, divided
1/2 c. buttery round crackers,
  crushed

Combine cream cheese, mayonnaise, Swiss cheese and onion.
Mix well; blend in half of the bacon. Spread in a small baking dish;
top with remaining bacon and crushed crackers. Bake at 350 degrees
for 15 minutes. Serve warm. Makes about 3 cups.

Carved pumpkins only stay fresh for a few days. To keep them
fresh longer, coat the cut edges with petroleum jelly.

Cranberry-Almond Crunch Mix

Colleen McAleavey
Pittsburgh, PA

Family & friends won't be able to stop nibbling on this!

12 c. popped popcorn
1 c. brown sugar, packed
1/2 c. butter
1/2 c. light corn syrup
1/2 t. salt

1/2 t. baking soda
1 c. whole almonds or
    honey-roasted peanuts
2 c. sweetened, dried cranberries
1-1/2 c. white chocolate chips

Place popcorn in a very large bowl or roasting pan; set aside. Combine brown sugar, butter, corn syrup and salt in a heavy saucepan. Cook over medium heat for 5 to 6 minutes, stirring constantly, until edges bubble and mixture reaches the soft-crack stage, or 270 to 289 degrees on a candy thermometer. Remove from heat; stir in baking soda. Pour mixture over popcorn; stir to coat. Add nuts, cranberries and chocolate chips; mix well. Pour onto baking sheets sprayed with non-stick vegetable spray. Bake for one hour at 250 degrees, stirring every 10 to 15 minutes. Spread on wax paper to cool. Store in an airtight container. Makes about 17 cups.

Whip up a simple rustic centerpiece...fill an old-fashioned colander or vintage baking pan with colorful apples. They're perfect for snacking on too!

Creamy Apple Cider Dip

Crystal Finnegan
Hastings, NE

This is the best! Slice favorite fruits or cubes of gingerbread or pumpkin bread for dipping.

4 c. apple cider
1/2 vanilla bean, split
1-1/2 c. sugar

1 t. lemon juice
2 T. butter
2 T. whipping cream

Combine cider and vanilla bean in a saucepan; simmer for 30 minutes over medium heat until reduced to one cup. Stir in sugar and lemon juice; cook for 10 minutes, or until mixture turns deep amber in color. Remove from heat; discard vanilla bean. Mix in butter and cream. Makes 2-1/2 cups.

Tasty appetizers in a snap. Just spoon soft cream cheese into celery and top with spiced pecans.

Herb-Seasoned Spinach Balls

Pat Habiger
Spearville, KS

Trust me...even the kids will love 'em!

2 10-oz. pkgs. frozen chopped
    spinach
1 T. dried, minced onion
2 c. herb-flavored stuffing mix

1 c. grated Parmesan cheese
2 eggs, beaten
3 T. butter, melted

Cook spinach and onion together according to package instructions; drain well. Place spinach mixture in a mixing bowl. Add stuffing mix and cheese, blending well. Add eggs and butter, mixing well again; shape into one-inch balls. Arrange in a lightly greased 13"x9" baking pan. Bake at 375 degrees for 15 to 20 minutes, until firm and golden. Makes 8 to 10 servings.

I cannot endure to waste anything as precious as autumn sunshine by staying in the house. So I spend almost all the daylight hours in the open air.

-Nathaniel Hawthorne

Sausage-Sauerkraut Balls

Karen Puchnick
Butler, PA

These are always a huge hit! I created my own recipe, mixing and matching other recipes until I found one I really liked.

1/2 lb. ground pork sausage
1/4 c. onion, finely chopped
2 c. sauerkraut, drained and
   chopped
1 c. plus 2 T. dry bread crumbs,
   divided
3-oz. pkg. cream cheese,
   softened
2 T. dried parsley
1 t. mustard

1/8 t. garlic salt
1/8 t. celery salt
1/8 t. pepper
2 eggs
1/4 c. milk
1/2 to 1 c. all-purpose flour
oil for deep frying
Optional: barbecue sauce or
   other dipping sauce

Cook sausage and onion together in a skillet until meat is browned; drain. Add sauerkraut and 2 tablespoons bread crumbs; set aside. Combine cream cheese and seasonings in a bowl; mix well. Stir cream cheese mixture into sausage mixture; chill for 2 hours to overnight. Shape into one-inch balls; set aside. Beat together eggs and milk in a small bowl; place flour and remaining bread crumbs in 2 separate small bowls. Coat sauerkraut balls with flour; dip into egg mixture and roll in crumbs. Deep-fry balls in hot oil until golden; place on a baking sheet and bake at 375 degrees for 15 to 20 minutes. Serve with dipping sauce, if desired. Makes 3 to 4 dozen.

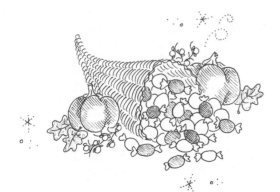

For an unexpected surprise, fill a harvest cornucopia with candies wrapped in harvest colors.

Antipasto

Doreen DeRosa
New Castle, PA

A super, make-ahead recipe.

1 green pepper, chopped
1 hot or mild pepper, sliced
   into rings
16-oz. pkg. sliced mushrooms
1 lb. hard salami, cubed
1/2 lb. pepperoni, cubed
1 onion, chopped

16-oz. pkg. brick cheese, cubed
16-oz. pkg. provolone cheese,
   cubed
6-oz. can black olives, drained
   and sliced
1-1/2 c. Italian salad dressing

Toss together all ingredients in a serving bowl. Cover and chill overnight. Serves 12.

Philly Dip

Melanie Evert
Denver, PA

In the Philadelphia region, everyone knows and loves hoagies.
This recipe combines all the flavors of a hoagie into
a hearty dip. I love it with French or Italian bread.

1/2 lb. Genoa salami
1/2 lb. cooked ham
1/2 lb. American cheese
1 onion

1 head lettuce
2 tomatoes, diced
1/2 c. mayonnaise

Use a food processor or knife to finely chop first 5 ingredients. Combine all ingredients; mix well. Add mayonnaise as needed for desired consistency. Makes about 5 to 6 cups.

Italian Meatballs

Shari Miller
Hobart, IN

*So versatile...these can be served as an appetizer, over pasta
or rice, or even make great sub sandwiches.*

2 lbs. ground beef
2 c. seasoned dry bread crumbs
1 c. milk
1/4 c. dried, minced onion
2 t. garlic salt

1/4 t. pepper
8-oz. pkg. mozzarella cheese
1/3 c. all-purpose flour
1/4 c. oil
4 15-oz. jars pizza sauce

Combine ground beef, bread crumbs, milk, onion, garlic salt and
pepper in a bowl just until mixed. Shape into 48 small meatballs; set
aside. Cut cheese into 48, 1/2-inch cubes. Push a cheese cube into the
center of each meatball, covering the cheese completely. Roll meatballs
lightly in flour. Heat oil in a large skillet and cook meatballs just until
browned; drain. Add pizza sauce to skillet. Bring to a boil over medium
heat; reduce heat, cover and simmer for 25 to 30 minutes, or until
meatballs are no longer pink. Makes 4 dozen.

Give a creepy, crawly Halloween touch to a buffet table of
appetizers. There's nothing like bugs crawling up and across
the tablecloth...plastic ones, that is! "Bugs" secure
and remove easily with double-stick tape.

Apple & Brie Toasts

Jo Ann

Everyone loves this!

1 loaf French bread, thinly sliced
1/4 c. butter, melted
1/2 c. brown sugar, packed
1/2 c. chopped walnuts

13.2-oz. pkg. Brie cheese,
  thinly sliced
3 Granny Smith apples,
  cored and sliced

Arrange bread on an ungreased baking sheet; bake at 350 degrees until lightly toasted. Set aside. Mix together butter, sugar and walnuts. Top each slice of bread with a cheese slice, an apple slice and a teaspoonful of butter mixture. Return to baking sheet; bake briefly until cheese melts. Makes 24 to 30.

Nibble appetizers outside on the porch or deck harvest-style. Light tables with tealights placed in hollowed-out apples, arrange hay bales for casual seating and fill sap buckets with sprays of bittersweet.

Maple-Topped Sweet Potato Skins
Linda Corcoran
Metuchen, NJ

I love finding these on a buffet table...they're absolutely wonderful!

6 large sweet potatoes
1/2 c. cream cheese, softened
1/4 c. sour cream
2 t. cinnamon, divided
2 t. nutmeg, divided
2 t. ground ginger, divided

2 c. chopped walnuts or pecans
3 T. butter, softened
1/4 c. brown sugar, packed
Garnish: maple syrup, apple
slices, additional nuts

Pierce potatoes with a fork. Bake at 400 degrees or microwave on high setting until tender; cool. Slice each potato in half lengthwise; scoop out baked insides, keeping skins intact. Mash baked potato in a mixing bowl until smooth; add cream cheese, sour cream and one teaspoon each of spices. Mix well and spoon into potato skins. Mix nuts, butter, brown sugar and remaining spices; sprinkle over top. Place potato skins on an ungreased baking sheet; bake at 400 degrees for 15 minutes. Drizzle with warm syrup; garnish as desired. Serves 12.

Host a family reunion this fall...the weather is almost always picture-perfect! When sending invitations, be sure to encourage everyone to bring photos, recipes, videos, scrapbooks and anything that inspires memories.

Tailgating Tortilla Wrap-Ups

Sue Stough
Madison, AL

Be sure to plan ahead...these need to chill 24 hours before serving.

8-oz. pkg. cream cheese,
  softened
1/2 c. sour cream
1/3 c. green onion, chopped
1/4 lb. smoked turkey or cooked
  ham, finely shredded

8-oz. pkg. finely shredded
  Cheddar cheese
seasoned salt to taste
Optional: black olives, chopped
4 to 5 10-inch flour tortillas

Combine all ingredients except tortillas until well blended. Spread on top of each tortilla; roll up. Wrap with plastic wrap; refrigerate for 24 hours. At serving time, slice into one-inch thick pieces. Makes about 48.

Buffalo Wing Chip Dip

Cyndy DeStefano
Mercer, PA

Each year I make these for tailgating get-togethers and television football games. They're really terrific!

2 10-oz. cans chicken, drained
8-oz. pkg. cream cheese,
  softened
1 c. shredded Cheddar cheese

1/3 c. hot pepper sauce
1/4 c. blue cheese salad dressing
Optional: 1/2 c. crumbled
  blue cheese

Mix together all ingredients; place in a 1-1/2 quart casserole dish sprayed lightly with non-stick vegetable spray. Bake for 30 to 35 minutes at 350 degrees. Makes about 5 cups.

Fall is the ideal time to plant spring flowering
bulbs! Plant them in October, when the weather is cool
and stays cool.

HAY-DAY Appetizers

Artichoke-Garlic Dip

Carole Larkins
Elmendorf AFB, AK

*Serve this up in a hollowed-out squash and enjoy with
warm sourdough bread or hearty crackers.*

14-oz. can artichokes, drained
    and chopped
1/2 c. grated Parmesan cheese
8-oz. pkg. cream cheese,
    softened

1/2 c. mayonnaise
1/2 t. dill weed
2 cloves garlic, minced
Optional: grated Parmesan
    cheese

Combine all ingredients in an ungreased 10" pie plate. If desired,
sprinkle with additional Parmesan cheese. Bake at 400 degrees for
15 minutes, or until golden. Makes about 3-1/2 cups.

Texas 2-Step Guacamole

Shirley Beth Fraley
Katy, TX

One taste will have you dancing!

2 avocados, peeled
    and pitted
1 T. lime juice
1 tomato, finely chopped

2 T. onion, minced
1/2 t. coriander
1/2 t. salt
Optional: 1 T. picante sauce

Mash avocados with a fork. Add remaining ingredients; mix well.
Cover and refrigerate before serving. Makes 1-1/2 cups.

An open home, an open heart,
here grows a bountiful harvest.

-Judy Hand

Harvest Moon Caramel Corn

Kendra Guinn
Smithville, TN

A family favorite during movie time at home.

24 to 32 c. popped popcorn
1 c. margarine
2 c. brown sugar, packed
1/2 c. corn syrup

1/2 t. salt
1 t. vanilla extract
1/2 t. baking soda

Place popcorn in a large roaster pan that has been sprayed with non-stick vegetable spray; set aside. Combine margarine, brown sugar, corn syrup and salt in a heavy saucepan over medium heat. Bring to a boil over medium heat; cook for 5 minutes. Remove from heat. Add vanilla and baking soda; stir well and pour over popcorn. Mix well; bake at 250 degrees for one hour, stirring occasionally. Let cool; break up and store in an airtight container. Makes 24 to 32 cups.

Howling Good Snack Mix

Carol Gibson
Lexington, KY

A terrific treat to share on Halloween!

1/2 c. wild berries
(red jelly beans)
1/2 c. owl rings (doughnut-shaped oat cereal)
1/2 c. colored flies (candy-coated chocolates)
1/2 c. butterfly wings
(corn chips)
1/2 c. ants (raisins)

1/2 c. cobwebs (sweetened flaked coconut)
1/2 c. earthworms (chow mein noodles)
1/2 c. squirrels' nuts (peanuts)
1/2 c. bat bones (mini pretzels)
1/2 c. birdseed (sunflower kernels)

Mix all ingredients together in a large bowl; store in an airtight container. Makes about 5 to 6 cups.

HAY-DAY
Appetizers

Sweet & Spicy Pecans

Sharon Miller
Dallas, TX

I usually double or triple this recipe. Just be sure to use several baking sheets to keep nuts in a single layer.

1/4 c. plus 2 T. sugar, divided
1 c. warm water
1 c. pecan halves

1 T. chili powder
1/4 t. cinnamon
1/8 t. cayenne pepper

Stir together 1/4 cup sugar and warm water until sugar dissolves. Add pecans; let stand 10 minutes. Drain, discarding liquid. Combine remaining sugar and spices; toss with pecans to coat. Spread pecans in a single layer on a lightly greased baking sheet. Bake at 350 degrees for 10 minutes, stirring once. Let cool; store in an airtight container. Makes one cup.

For a clever serving idea, line vintage lunch or
trick-or-treat pails with wax paper and fill with
easy-to-nibble appetizers, nuts or candies.

Old-Fashioned Kettle Corn

Teresa Hinrichsen
North Mankato, MN

This is a homemade version of the sweet & salty
kettle corn found at so many fall festivals.

2 T. sunflower oil
1/2 c. unpopped popcorn

1/4 c. raw sugar
1/2 t. salt

Place first 3 ingredients in a hand-cranked popcorn popper. Cook popcorn mixture over medium-high heat while turning the crank. Alternatively, cook popcorn mixture in a large stockpot with lid, shaking to pop corn. Once kernels begin to pop, reduce heat to low and continue cranking or shaking until popping stops. Place popcorn in a large bowl; sprinkle with salt. Makes 12 cups.

Thanksgiving Harvest Mix

Jo Ann Belovitch
Stratford, CT

So nice to serve in individual Thanksgiving baking cups or candy
cups...place one on each plate at Thanksgiving dinner.

12-oz. pkg. candy corn
12-oz. pkg. mixed dried fruit

10-oz. pkg. sunflower kernels

Mix all ingredients together; store in an airtight container.
Makes 4 to 5 cups.

White Chocolate Party Mix

Karen Pilcher
Burleson, TX

A yummy school lunchbox treat.

10-oz. pkg. mini pretzels
5 c. doughnut-shaped oat cereal
5 c. bite-size crispy corn
   cereal squares
2 c. salted peanuts

14-oz. pkg. candy-coated
   chocolates
2 12-oz. pkgs. white
   chocolate chips
3 T. oil

Combine pretzels, cereals, peanuts and candy-coated chocolates in a large bowl; set aside. Place chocolate chips and oil in a microwave-safe bowl; microwave on medium-high setting for 2 minutes, stirring once. Microwave again for 10 seconds; stir until smooth. Pour over pretzel mixture; mix well. Spread onto 3 to 4 wax paper-lined baking sheets. Let cool; break apart and store in airtight containers. Makes 20 cups.

Frosted Pecans

Lisa Johnson
Hallsville, TX

With only 4 ingredients, this is ready to enjoy in no time. Spoon into little trick-or-treat bags and give to all the neighborhood kids.

1-1/2 c. sugar
1/2 c. sour cream

1-1/2 t. vanilla extract
1 lb. pecan pieces

Mix sugar and sour cream in a large saucepan; bring to a boil over medium heat and simmer for 5 minutes, stirring constantly. Add vanilla and pecans; stir until sugary and well-coated. Spread on wax paper; break into pieces when cool. Store in an airtight container. Makes 4 to 5 cups.

Share some favorite snacks with next-door friends...Good Neighbor Day is September 26th!

Pear & Blue Cheese Crostini

Lisa Ragland
Gooseberry Patch

A winning combination of flavors.

12 slices cocktail bread
1/4 c. mayonnaise
1 pear, cored, halved and thinly
   sliced

1/2 c. crumbled blue cheese
1/3 c. chopped pecans

Cut each slice of bread in half diagonally to form triangles. Place on an ungreased baking sheet; bake at 400 degrees for 4 to 5 minutes, until lightly toasted. Spread mayonnaise on bread; top with pear, blue cheese and pecans. Broil for 2 to 3 minutes, until cheese begins to melt. Makes 2 dozen.

Enjoy the best of the season...take a hayride, visit the apple orchard and pumpkin patch with family & friends. End the day gathered around a bonfire telling stories or singing songs.

Maple-Glazed Carrots

Kathy Grashoff
Fort Wayne, IN

A quick-to-fix side that goes nicely with any main dish.

16-oz. pkg. baby carrots
3 slices bacon, chopped
1 apple, cored, peeled and sliced
   into thin wedges

2 T. maple syrup
salt and pepper to taste

Place carrots in a saucepan and cover with water; bring to a boil over medium heat. Cook for 10 minutes, or until crisp-tender; drain. Set aside. Cook bacon in a skillet over medium heat for 3 minutes, or until lightly browned. Add apple and cook for 2 minutes. Add carrots, maple syrup, salt and pepper; stir frequently. Cook until carrots are warmed through and lightly glazed. Serve immediately. Serves 4.

The next time you take a walk in the garden,
bring along a small bag to collect leaves. The simplest way
to show off their colors in your home is to press them with a
warm iron between sheets of wax paper. When dry, simply
arrange them under a bell jar or in a glass goblet.

Cranberry-Yam Bake

Karen Van Loo
Pflugerville, TX

Everyone loves the sweetness combined with the slight tartness in this dish. It's become a family tradition to serve every Thanksgiving.

1/2 c. all-purpose flour
1/2 c. brown sugar, packed
1/2 c. quick-cooking oats,
   uncooked
1 t. cinnamon

1/3 c. butter, chilled
2 17-oz. cans yams, drained
   and slightly mashed
2 c. cranberries
1-1/2 c. mini marshmallows

Combine flour, brown sugar, oats and cinnamon in a large bowl. Cut in butter until mixture resembles coarse crumbs; set aside. Place yams and cranberries in another bowl; toss with one cup of crumb mixture. Arrange yam mixture in a lightly greased 1-1/2 quart casserole dish and sprinkle with remaining crumb mixture; bake at 350 degrees for 35 minutes. Sprinkle with marshmallows; broil until golden. Serves 6.

Enjoy an enchanted fall evening with the familiar crackle
and aroma of a campfire. A simple fire ring can be
made from a circle of large rocks. Toss a few handfuls
of kindling in the center, and once it begins to burn,
add some larger pieces of wood. Sit back and relax!

Candied-Glazed Baked Apples

Jackie Smulski
Lyons, IL

These apples have a little zip to them!

3/4 c. sugar
1/3 c. red cinnamon candies
1 c. water

4 baking apples
2 t. lemon juice
1 T. butter, diced

Combine sugar, cinnamon candies and water in a saucepan; bring to a boil, stirring until sugar dissolves. Reduce heat; simmer, uncovered, for 2 minutes. Remove from heat; set aside. Peel top third of each apple. Remove and discard core, leaving bottom intact. Brush top of apples with lemon juice; arrange in a lightly greased 8"x8" baking pan. Dot centers of apples with butter; brush generously with sugar-cinnamon glaze. Bake at 350 degrees, uncovered, for one hour; brush frequently with remaining sugar-cinnamon glaze. Serve warm. Serves 4.

If you're in a hurry to make gravy, try this super-simple method with your favorite recipe. Pour some of the pan drippings into a Mason jar. Add flour, tighten down the jar lid and shake well. Just pour back into the pan to finish cooking.

Creamy Butternut Squash

Rebecca Cook
San Antonio, TX

Carrots and onion add flavor to this classic fall side dish.

2 lbs. butternut squash, peeled
   and cubed
10-3/4 oz. can cream of
   chicken soup
8-oz. container sour cream

1/3 c. butter, melted
2 carrots, peeled and shredded
1/2 c. onion, chopped
2-1/4 c. herb-flavored stuffing
   mix, divided

Place squash and a small amount of water in a saucepan. Simmer
for 3 minutes; drain well and set aside. Combine soup, sour cream,
butter, carrots and onion in a bowl; stir in 2 cups stuffing mix.
Fold in squash; transfer to a greased 11"x7" baking pan. Sprinkle
with remaining stuffing mix. Bake, uncovered, at 350 degrees for
45 minutes. Serves 4 to 6.

When it comes to carving squash, try using the knife
that comes in a pumpkin carving kit...its little size
is just right for slicing squash!

Corn Soufflé

Jan Ramsey
Wellington, TX

A super-simple dish that can be made in a flash.

1/4 c. margarine
1/4 c. all-purpose flour
1 t. salt
2 T. sugar

1-3/4 c. milk
3 eggs, beaten
3 c. frozen corn, cooked and
   drained

Mix margarine, flour, salt and sugar in a saucepan; add milk. Cook and stir over medium heat until thickened; remove from heat. Stir in eggs and corn; pour into a greased 1-1/2 quart casserole dish. Bake at 350 degrees for 45 minutes. Serves 4 to 6.

Nut & Honey Potato Salad

Sandy Bernards
Valencia, CA

Try this new spin on traditional potato salad...you'll love it!

1-1/2 c. mayonnaise
1/4 c. brown sugar, packed
2 T. applesauce
2 T. cinnamon
2 T. honey

2 T. maple syrup
1-1/2 lbs. sweet potatoes,
   peeled, boiled and diced
8-oz. pkg. chopped pecans,
   toasted

Combine all ingredients except sweet potatoes and pecans in a large bowl; mix well. Add potatoes and pecans; toss well to mix. Chill for several hours before serving. Serves 4 to 6.

Everyone must take time
to sit and watch the
leaves turn.

- Elizabeth Lawrence

Caramel Apple Salad

Kristen Dolan
La Mesa, CA

This is so delicious! Guaranteed to disappear quickly.

8-oz. container frozen whipped
  topping, thawed
3-1/2 oz. pkg. instant
  butterscotch pudding mix

8-oz. can crushed pineapple
3 c. apples, cored and diced
1 c. dry-roasted peanuts
1 c. mini marshmallows

Mix whipped topping, pudding mix and pineapple together; add
remaining ingredients. Refrigerate until ready to serve. Serves 8.

Apple & Cranberry Sauce

Abby Hines
Winston-Salem, NC

The more you stir, the more like applesauce this will become.
If you like a thicker sauce, don't stir as much.

4 Granny Smith apples,
  cored, peeled and sliced
1/2 c. sweetened, dried
  cranberries
2 T. brown sugar, packed

1 t. cinnamon
1/2 t. nutmeg
1 T. cornstarch
1/2 c. water

Place apples, cranberries, brown sugar and nutmeg in a saucepan.
Cover and simmer over medium heat until apples are tender, about
15 to 20 minutes. Remove from heat; let cool until no longer boiling.
Dissolve cornstarch in water; stir into apple mixture. Cook over
medium-low heat just until thickened. Serve warm. Makes 4 servings.

Autumn...the year's last,
  loveliest smile.

-William Cullen Bryant

Cornmeal Dumplings

Nichole Martelli
Alvin, TX

My grandmother shared this recipe with me a few years ago and it's been a favorite ever since. I can't help but think of her every time I make this. These are wonderful in any stew and make a tasty side for roasts.

1/2 to 1-lb. meaty ham bone	2 eggs, beaten
1 c. cornmeal	1 onion, chopped
1 c. all-purpose flour	salt and pepper to taste

Place ham bone in a stockpot; cover with water. Bring to a boil and cook until meat is tender. Remove meat from bone and return meat to stockpot. Mix remaining ingredients together with just enough ham broth to make a dough. Roll out dough 1/4-inch thick; cut into strips and drop into simmering ham broth. Simmer over low heat for about 10 minutes, or until they rise to the top. Remove dumplings and meat to serve. Serves 6 to 8.

Try this with colorful fall apples...clever photo holders!
Glue a tiny clothespin to the end of a short, thin stick; let dry.
Insert the opposite end of the stick into the top of an apple.
Pinch clothespins open and insert photos.

FARMSTAND-FRESH
Sides & Salads

Hearty Macaroni & Cheese

Elizabeth King
McFarland, WI

A great recipe for leftover turkey from Thanksgiving.

1-1/2 c. elbow macaroni,
   uncooked
3 T. butter
2 T. all-purpose flour
1/4 t. salt
1/8 t. pepper
2 c. milk
1/4 c. onion, finely chopped
8-oz. pkg. shredded sharp
   Cheddar cheese

2 c. cooked chicken or
   turkey, chopped
4 eggs, hard-boiled, peeled
   and chopped
1 c. peas
1 c. Italian-seasoned
   bread crumbs

Cook macaroni according to package instructions; drain. Melt butter in
a saucepan; blend in flour, salt and pepper. Add milk; cook over
medium heat, stirring constantly, until thick and bubbly. Add onion
and cheese; cook until melted. Mix cheese sauce with macaroni; add
chicken or turkey, eggs and peas. Pour into a 1-1/2 quart casserole
dish sprayed lightly with non-stick vegetable spray. Top with bread
crumbs; bake at 350 degrees, uncovered, for 35 to 40 minutes.
Serves 6 to 8.

Head to the apple orchard
for a fall feast. After
lunch, pick a bushel or 2
of apples to take
home...farm-fresh and
perfect for
homemade treats!

Cheddar-Colby Pasta Bake

Lynda Sommerville
Newville, PA

This gets better the more you reheat it...super for quick meals!

3 c. prepared elbow macaroni
8-oz. pkg. shredded sharp
　Cheddar cheese
1 c. shredded Colby-Jack cheese
1/4 c. butter, melted

1 c. milk
salt and pepper to taste
1 green pepper, chopped
1 tomato, chopped

Combine macaroni, cheeses, butter, milk, salt and pepper in a greased
2-1/2 quart casserole dish. Add green pepper and tomato; mix gently.
Bake at 350 degrees, covered, for one hour. Uncover and bake an
additional 30 minutes. Serves 6.

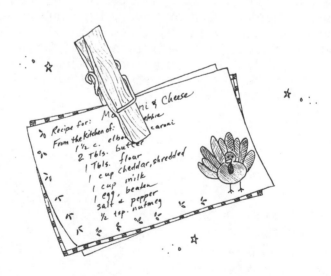

Pick up a bunch of clip-style clothespins...just right
in the kitchen as "chip clips." They come in handy for
clipping together recipes or coupons too.

Carrots Au Gratin

Carol Sageser
Greensburg, IN

Delightfully easy and deliciously cheesy.

3 c. carrots, peeled and sliced
10-3/4 oz. can cream of
    celery soup

1 c. shredded Cheddar cheese
1/4 c. dry bread crumbs
1 T. butter, melted

Place carrots in a saucepan. Cover with water and cook over medium heat until crisp-tender; drain. Combine carrots, soup and cheese in a one-quart casserole dish lightly sprayed with non-stick vegetable spray; set aside. Mix bread crumbs and butter; sprinkle over carrot mixture. Bake at 350 degrees for 20 to 25 minutes. Serves 6.

Look for decorative shoe buckles at the next junk sale or flea market...they make whimsical napkin holders! Just slip some ribbon through the buckle and tie around a rolled-up napkin.

Creamed Spinach Casserole

Debi DeVore
Dover, OH

This recipe is easily doubled.
Bake in a shallow 2-quart baking dish.

10-oz. pkg. frozen chopped
   spinach
1/4 c. plus 1 T. butter, divided
1/2 t. salt
1/4 t. pepper

1/2 c. shredded Cheddar cheese
2 eggs, beaten
1/2 c. milk
1/2 c. soft bread crumbs

In a saucepan over medium heat, cook spinach with a small amount of water for 2 to 3 minutes. Drain thoroughly. Add 1/4 cup butter, salt, pepper, cheese, eggs and milk. Spoon into 2 greased ramekins. Melt remaining butter and mix with crumbs. Sprinkle over spinach mixture. Bake, uncovered, at 350 degrees for 25 to 30 minutes, or until almost set. Serves 2.

Set out a variety of games and puzzles for when family & friends are visiting. Pull out your childhood favorites...sure to spark memories and laughter.

Old-Fashioned Cheese Bake

Joy Hawkins
Cherokee, OR

Keep this on hand for the holiday buffet table...a tried & true dish.

10 slices bread, cubed
1/2 c. butter, melted
2 c. milk
3 eggs, separated
1 t. dry mustard

1/2 c. shredded sharp Cheddar
  cheese
1/2 t. salt
1/2 t. cayenne pepper

Toss together bread and butter. Stir in milk and beaten egg yolks. Add mustard, cheese, salt and cayenne pepper; mix well. Beat egg whites until stiff peaks form; fold into bread mixture. Spoon into a greased 13"x9" baking pan; cover and refrigerate for at least 12 hours. Bake at 350 degrees for 50 minutes. Serves 8 to 10.

Cooler weather and longer evenings are a cozy time just right for curling up with a good book. Keep several of your favorites on a table next to a cozy chair, brew a cup of herbal tea and sit back to enjoy.

Sour Cream Potatoes

Amanda Zuech
Franklinville, NY

These potatoes disappear fast from the dinner table!

6 to 8 potatoes, peeled and cubed	1 T. butter, softened
8-oz. container sour cream	1/2 c. milk
1/2 c. cream cheese, softened	1 t. garlic powder
	1 c. shredded Cheddar cheese

Cover potatoes with water and boil until tender; drain and set aside. Blend together remaining ingredients except Cheddar cheese; stir into warm potatoes. Spread in a 13"x9" baking pan lightly sprayed with non-stick vegetable spray; sprinkle with Cheddar cheese. Cover and bake for about one hour at 325 degrees. Serve immediately. Makes 8 to 10 servings.

Quilts, buffalo check blankets and
blanket-stitched throws make the best spreads for
an outdoor picnic or tailgating get-together.

Golden Cornbread Dressing

Charlotte Wolfe
Fort Lauderdale, FL

*When squash is at its most abundant in the fall,
try this recipe. Sure to please!*

1 c. yellow squash, sliced
1 onion, chopped
1 c. cornbread, crumbled

10-3/4 oz. can cream of
chicken soup

Combine squash and onion in a saucepan with a small amount of water. Steam just until tender; drain. Combine squash mixture with cornbread and soup; spread in a greased 8"x8" baking pan. Bake at 350 degrees for 35 to 40 minutes. Serves 4 to 6.

Serving up baked potatoes with dinner?
Rub the skins with butter and salt
before baking...so delicious!

Loaded Mashed Potato Casserole

Tami Bowman
Gooseberry Patch

When you're in a pinch for time, speed up the prep for this casserole by using prepackaged mashed potatoes and bacon.

5-1/2 c. mashed potatoes
1/2 c. milk
8-oz. pkg. cream cheese, softened
8-oz. container sour cream
2 t. dried parsley

1 t. garlic salt
1/4 t. nutmeg
3/4 c. shredded Cheddar cheese
1/2 c. bacon, crisply cooked and crumbled

Combine all ingredients except cheese and bacon in a large bowl. Blend with an electric mixer on medium-high setting until smooth. Spoon into a lightly greased 13"x9" baking pan; top with cheese and bacon. Cover and bake at 350 degrees for 30 minutes, until heated through. Makes 12 servings.

Keep side dishes warm by spooning into the top of a double boiler. Fill the bottom of the double boiler with water and simmer over very low heat.

Cauliflower Au Gratin

Lore Griffiths
Frankfort, IL

The mustard gives this side a great taste!

1 head cauliflower, greens
   removed
1/2 c. mayonnaise

2 t. mustard
3/4 c. shredded Cheddar cheese

Steam whole cauliflower until tender. Drain and place in a lightly greased 8"x8" baking pan; keep warm. Mix remaining ingredients; spread over top and sides of cauliflower. Place under broiler for 3 to 5 minutes, until cheese mixture starts to bubble. Serve immediately. Makes 6 servings.

A delicious drizzle for steamed veggies!
Boil 1/2 cup balsamic vinegar, stirring often,
until thickened. So simple and scrumptious.

Scalloped Oyster Stuffing

Brittany Thorngren
Broomfield, CO

This will be your new favorite way to prepare stuffing!

1/2 c. onion, diced
1 c. celery, thinly sliced
1 c. margarine, softened
2 8-oz. cans oysters, drained
    and liquid reserved
1 c. whipping cream

1/4 c. fresh parsley, chopped
1/2 t. salt
1/4 t. pepper
3 3-1/2 oz. pkgs. unsalted soda
    crackers, coarsely crushed

Sauté onion and celery in margarine in a skillet over medium heat until soft. Remove from heat; stir in oyster liquid, cream, parsley, salt and pepper. Set aside. Combine oysters and cracker crumbs in a large bowl; spoon onion mixture over top and toss lightly to mix. Let stand 5 minutcs, until liquid is absorbed. Cover and chill until ready to use. Makes enough to fill a 16 to 18-pound turkey. Serves 5 to 7.

Fill a hollowed-out pumpkin with stuffing, veggies or salad...they look darling on a buffet table.

Cheesy Rice & Veggies

Robin Guyor
Berkley, MI

*You can serve this as a side dish, as I do, or as a main dish.
Either way, it's a winner!*

3 c. prepared rice
10-oz. pkg. frozen corn
8-oz. pkg. shredded sharp
   Cheddar cheese
1/3 c. onion, chopped
1/2 green pepper, chopped

1/2 red pepper, chopped
1/2 c. milk
1/2 t. taco seasoning mix
1/2 t. salt
1/8 t. pepper
Garnish: paprika

Combine all ingredients except paprika in a large mixing bowl.
Mix well and pour into a greased 2-quart casserole dish. Sprinkle with
paprika. Bake at 350 degrees for 45 minutes, or until golden and
bubbly on top. Makes 6 to 8 servings.

Have an "It's back-to-school time!" dinner
especially for the kids. Set a table outside and serve up all
their favorite foods. For dessert, build a bonfire,
roast apples and make s'mores.

Scalloped Apples

Jacqueline Kurtz
Reading, PA

A super-simple microwave recipe.

10 tart apples, cored, peeled
   and sliced
1/3 c. sugar
2 T. cornstarch

1/2 to 1 t. cinnamon
1/8 t. nutmeg
2 T. butter, cubed

Place apples in a 2-1/2 quart microwave-safe bowl lightly sprayed
with non-stick vegetable spray; set aside. Combine sugar, cornstarch
and spices; sprinkle over apples and toss to coat. Dot with butter.
Cover and microwave on high setting for 15 minutes, or until apples
are tender, stirring every 5 minutes. Serves 6.

Spicy Fruit & Bread Stuffing

Gail Prather
Lakeside, CA

One of the most delicious stuffing recipes.

2 c. dry bread crumbs
1 c. celery, sliced
1/4 c. butter, melted
1/4 c. chicken broth
4-oz. pkg. whole mixed dried
   fruit, halved

1 onion, chopped
1/2 t. salt
1/4 t. pepper
1/4 t. cinnamon
1/8 t. ground cloves
1/8 t. ground ginger

Mix all ingredients together; stir until well combined. Spoon stuffing
into a lightly greased 2-quart casserole dish. Bake, covered, at
375 degrees for about 30 minutes, or use to stuff a 4 to 5-pound
chicken. Serves 4.

A slow cooker filled with cider, a sprinkle of cinnamon and
orange slices is perfect for harvest get-togethers!

Honey-Kissed Acorn Squash

Lynda McCormick
Burkburnett, TX

This fresh side dish is a great addition to any dinner menu.

2 acorn squash, halved
   lengthwise and seeded
3 T. honey
1/4 c. butter, melted
2 T. chopped pecans

2 T. sweetened, dried cranberries
   or cherries
2 T. crushed pineapple
Garnish: nutmeg

Place squash halves cut-side up in a microwave-safe dish; cook on high setting until tender, about 8 to 10 minutes. Combine remaining ingredients except nutmeg; spoon into squash halves. Microwave on high setting for 30 to 45 seconds, until heated through and lightly glazed. Sprinkle with nutmeg. Serves 4.

The earth has rolled around again and harvest time is here.

-Carolyn Wells

Mom's Sausage Dressing

Laurie Michael
Colorado Springs, CO

Mom always made sausage dressing at Thanksgiving
when I was growing up. Being from the south, she made it with
cornbread. I always get lots of compliments when
I serve it to my family & friends.

1/2 c. butter
2 stalks celery, chopped
1 onion, chopped
5 c. cornbread, crumbled
3 c. day-old white bread, cubed
1/2 T. poultry seasoning
1/2 T. dried sage
1 t. salt

1 t. pepper
1 lb. ground pork sausage,
   browned and drained
2 14-1/2 oz. cans chicken broth
10-3/4 oz. can cream of
   chicken soup
4 to 5 eggs, beaten

Melt butter in a skillet over medium heat. Add celery and onion; heat
until tender and set aside. Mix together breads and seasonings in a
large bowl. Add celery mixture, sausage, broth, soup, eggs and
enough water to make mixture soupy; mix well. Spoon into a greased
13"x9" baking pan. Bake, uncovered, at 350 degrees for 30 to
40 minutes, or until golden and heated through. Serves 8 to 10.

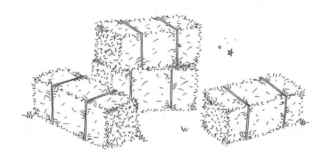

Create your own hay maze...it's simple. Stack bales of hay
or straw and make a little path that runs through them.
The kids will laugh all the way through it!

Mashed Cinnamon Sweet Potatoes *Brittany Butler*
Bowling Green, KY

*This recipe blends sweet potatoes with brown sugar and cinnamon
to create a delicious twist on mashed potatoes.*

40-oz. can sweet potatoes,
   drained and rinsed
1/2 c. butter, diced
1/4 c. brown sugar, packed

1-1/2 t. salt
3/4 t. cinnamon
1/8 t. white pepper

Combine all ingredients in a medium saucepan. Cook over medium
heat until butter melts. Mash with a potato masher until sweet
potatoes are smooth and all ingredients are well blended. Lower
heat; continue cooking until warmed through, about 5 minutes.
Serves 4 to 6.

Pitch a tent in the backyard on a fall night so the kids can
camp out, tell ghost stories and play flashlight tag.
What a way to make memories!

Cranberries & Spinach Salad

Judy Boettcher
Leavenworth, KS

Treat family & friends to this salad...it's almost too pretty to eat!

1/2 c. plus 1-1/2 T. sugar,
   divided
1 c. slivered almonds
16-oz. pkg. spinach, torn into
   bite-size pieces
1 c. sweetened, dried cranberries
1 T. toasted sesame seed

2 T. poppy seed
1/2 c. oil
1/4 c. white vinegar
1/4 c. cider vinegar
2 t. red onion, minced
1/4 t. paprika

Place 1-1/2 tablespoons sugar and almonds in a skillet; cook over medium heat until golden. Spread on wax paper to cool; break apart. Transfer to a bowl; stir in spinach and cranberries. Set aside. Mix remaining sugar, sesame seed, poppy seed, oil, vinegars, onion and paprika together; toss with spinach mixture. Serves 6 to 8.

An old trunk is ideal for filling with dress-up clothes
for scarecrow-making. Have a best-dressed
scarecrow contest while dinner's cooking!

FARMSTAND-FRESH
Sides & Salads

Mom's Cranberry Salad

Sherry Rich
Sun Valley, CA

For as long as I can remember, it was always a treat when my mom made this. It's absolutely delicious and can be made a day ahead.

16-oz. pkg. cranberries
1 c. whipping cream, whipped
15-1/4 oz. can crushed
    pineapple, drained

3 c. mini marshmallows
1-1/2 c. sugar

Grind cranberries in a food processor. Combine with remaining ingredients in a serving bowl. Cover and chill. Serves 8 to 10.

Mary's Nutty Greek Salad

Mary Baker
Georgetown, TX

I belong to a group of 12 neighborhood ladies who get together once a week for lunch...this salad is a favorite.

2 c. spinach, torn into bite-size
    pieces
1/3 c. red onion, thinly sliced
1 c. chopped pecans, toasted

1/2 c. crumbled feta cheese
1/4 c. red wine vinaigrette
1/3 c. green apple, cored and
    thinly sliced

Toss together spinach, onion, nuts and cheese; add vinaigrette to taste. Top with apple slices. Makes 2 servings.

Use decorative-edge scissors to trim around the edges of paper plates for a whimsical look.

Ham & Lima Bean Pot

LaVerne Fang
Joliet, IL

*Unbelievably good...a must-have for warming up
on a brisk day. So nice to tote to a church supper too.*

1-1/2 c. dried lima beans
6 c. water
1 c. cooked ham, diced
1 onion, chopped
1/3 c. molasses

1/3 c. chili sauce
1 T. vinegar
1 t. dry mustard
1/8 t. cayenne pepper

Combine beans and water in a stockpot; let stand overnight. Drain beans; add 6 cups fresh water. Simmer over low heat for 1-1/2 hours. Drain again, reserving one cup liquid. Combine cooked beans, reserved liquid and remaining ingredients. Mix well and spread in a lightly greased 2-quart casserole dish. Bake, uncovered, at 350 degrees for 30 minutes, or until golden. Makes 4 to 6 servings.

Fill vintage jelly jars with candy corn and
set a tealight inside each one. Their sweet glow will
make the prettiest place settings!

French-Style Green Bean Bake

Susan Desjardins
Rochester, NH

A dressed-up version of everybody's favorite green bean recipe.

10-3/4 can cream of
  chicken soup
1/2 c. milk
1/8 t. pepper
1 c. shredded mozzarella cheese,
  divided

10-oz. pkg. frozen French-style
  green beans, cooked and
  drained
2.8-oz can French fried onions,
  divided

In an ungreased 2-quart casserole dish, mix soup, milk, pepper and
1/2 cup cheese. Add green beans and half the onions. Bake at
350 degrees for 30 minutes. Remove from oven and stir mixture.
Top with remaining onions and sprinkle remaining cheese over the
onions. Bake for 5 additional minutes, until cheese melts.
Serves 6 to 8.

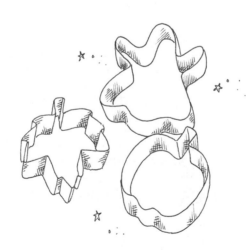

Use cookie cutters in leaf, pumpkin or ghost shapes to
cut out biscuit dough...a dinnertime surprise!

Jalapeño-Cheese Rice

Tammy Clark
Pampa, TX

Add a little kick to your sideboard sides!

4 cubes beef bouillon
4 c. boiling water
2 c. instant rice, uncooked
16-oz. pkg. pasteurized process
   cheese spread

1 T. onion, chopped
1/4 c. butter
1/2 c. oil
3 whole jalapeños

Dissolve bouillon in water; set aside. Prepare rice per package
instructions. Add bouillon and water; blend in remaining ingredients.
Serves 4 to 6.

Garlic & Herb Mashed Potatoes

Kathy Unruh
Fresno, CA

Everyone likes mashed potatoes...here's a new spin
they'll really enjoy. The herbs bring out the best flavor.

1 lb. new potatoes
5 cloves garlic
1/3 c. whipping cream
1 T. butter, softened

salt and pepper to taste
1 t. fresh rosemary, chopped
1 t. fresh marjoram, chopped
Garnish: fresh rosemary sprigs

Place potatoes and garlic in a large saucepan; cover with water. Boil
for 30 minutes, until potatoes are tender. Drain. Return potatoes and
garlic to saucepan; mash well. Add cream and butter; mix well. Add
salt and pepper; stir in herbs. Garnish with fresh rosemary sprigs.
Serves 6.

Sweet Potato Salad

Misty Swanson
Hendersonville, NC

This salad is a yummy mix of flavors.

2 lbs. sweet potatoes, peeled
  and cut into 1-inch cubes
3/4 t. salt, divided
1/2 c. onion, diced
1/3 c. green pepper, diced
3 T. brown sugar, packed
1 T. dried parsley

1/4 c. plus 1 T. white vinegar
1 T. oil
1 t. hot pepper sauce
1 t. mustard
3 slices bacon, crisply cooked
  and crumbled

Arrange sweet potatoes in an even layer on a baking sheet lightly sprayed with non-stick vegetable spray. Sprinkle potatoes with 1/2 teaspoon salt. Bake at 400 degrees for 25 minutes, or just until tender; let cool slightly. Stir together remaining ingredients except bacon until blended. Add potatoes and toss gently to coat; sprinkle with bacon. Serve warm or chilled. Serves 6 to 8.

Playing checkers has never been more fun! Purchase small craft store figurines shaped like pumpkins, turkeys, ghosts, apples and scarecrows. Use them instead of round game pieces for lots of giggles.

Country-Style Bean Bake

Lisa Ludwig
Fort Wayne, IN

A sure-fire hit for any get-together.

16-oz. can green beans, drained
16-oz. can wax beans, drained
4-oz. can sliced mushrooms,
    drained

8-oz. can tomato sauce
1/4 c. grated Parmesan cheese
3 T. butter, melted
1/2 t. salt

Combine beans and mushrooms in a lightly greased 1-1/2 quart casserole dish; set aside. Mix together remaining ingredients; pour over bean mixture. Stir well. Bake at 350 degrees for 25 minutes. Makes 4 to 6 servings.

Bacon-Topped Veggie Bake

Cheri Emery
Quincy, IL

The perfect match...broccoli, corn and bacon.

10-oz. pkg. frozen chopped
    broccoli
1 egg, beaten
14-3/4 oz. can creamed corn
1/4 c. margarine, melted

2 slices bread, toasted, buttered
    and cubed
3 slices bacon, crisply cooked
    and crumbled

Cook broccoli according to package directions; drain well. Combine with egg, corn and margarine. Mix well; place in a lightly greased 1-1/2 quart casserole dish. Bake, covered, at 350 degrees for 40 minutes. Top with cubed toast and crumbled bacon; bake, uncovered, an additional 20 minutes. Serves 4 to 6.

Follow your bliss.

-Joseph Campbell

Best-Ever Onion Casserole

Jennifer Ordway
Wichita, KS

A great addition to any meal...all the flavors of French onion soup.

4 onions, sliced
3 T. butter
2 T. all-purpose flour
1 c. beef broth

1/4 c. dry sherry or beef broth
1-1/2 c. croutons
1/4 c. shredded Swiss cheese
2 T. grated Parmesan cheese

Cook onions in butter over medium heat until soft. Add flour; cook and stir until thickened and smooth. Add broth and sherry or broth; cook until bubbly. Pour into a lightly greased 13"x9" baking pan; bake at 350 degrees for 30 minutes. Sprinkle with croutons and cheeses. Bake an additional 5 minutes, until cheeses are melted. Serves 4 to 6.

On a crisp, sunny day, take your family on a hike to the woods. Pick up colorful leaves, acorns, walnuts and bittersweet. Come home and string a fall garland to hang across the mantel or doorway.

Golden Homestyle Rice

Marcia Emig
Goodland, KS

So tasty, I like it as a change of pace from potato side dishes.

1 c. long-cooking rice, uncooked
1/2 c. green onion, chopped
1 T. butter
8-oz. pkg. sliced mushrooms
1-1/2 c. chicken broth

1/2 c. dry sherry or
    chicken broth
1 t. salt
1 t. pepper

Pour rice into a greased 11"x7" baking pan; set aside. Sauté onion with butter in a medium saucepan until soft. Add mushrooms; continue to sauté until mushrooms are soft. Pour in chicken broth, sherry or broth, salt and pepper; bring to a boil. Remove from heat and pour over rice in baking pan. Cover and bake at 375 degrees for 25 to 30 minutes. Makes 4 servings.

A vintage black lunchbox makes a clever
Halloween candy holder...just fill with tasty treats
for little goblins to choose from.

Country-Style
Soups & Breads

Woods Creek Bean Soup

Connie West
Sonora, CA

*I think this is best with thick slices of warm sourdough bread
and a simple apple and raisin salad.*

1 c. baby carrots, halved
1 c. onion, chopped
2 cloves garlic, minced
7-oz. pkg. turkey Kielbasa,
   halved lengthwise and cut
   into 1/2-inch pieces

4 c. fat-free chicken broth
1/2 t. Italian seasoning
1/2 t. pepper
15.8-oz. can Great Northern
   beans, drained and rinsed
6-oz. pkg. baby spinach

Place carrots, onion, garlic and Kielbasa in a large saucepan coated
with non-stick vegetable spray. Sauté over medium-high heat for
about 4 minutes, stirring occasionally. Lower heat; cook an additional
5 minutes. Add broth, Italian seasoning, pepper and beans. Bring to a
boil; reduce heat and simmer 5 minutes. Place 2 cups of soup in a food
processor or blender and process until smooth. Return puréed mixture
to pan; simmer an additional 5 minutes. Remove soup from heat; add
spinach, stirring carefully until spinach wilts. Serves 5.

Give your crackling fire a fragrant touch...toss in
a handful of dried herbs from the garden.
Sage and lavender are particularly nice.

Cranberry-Buttermilk Bread

Vicki Hale
Lexington, KY

Spread with butter and enjoy this sweeter,
lighter version of cornbread.

2 c. self-rising cornmeal
1/2 c. self-rising flour
1 c. sugar
1 egg, beaten

1/2 c. cranberries, chopped
2 c. buttermilk
1/4 c. shortening, melted

Mix cornmeal, flour, sugar, egg, cranberries and buttermilk in a large bowl; add melted shortening. Mix well. Pour into a greased 9"x5" loaf pan to one inch below the rim. Bake at 350 degrees for approximately one hour, or until golden. Makes one loaf.

When taking soup to a reunion or tailgating get-together, it's easy to keep it warm. Preheat a thermos by filling it with hot water for about 10 minutes, empty, then add hot soup.

Chicken & Dumpling Soup

Linda Nagy
Marine City, MI

*Fill a quart-size Mason jar with this hearty soup and tuck into a
"sniffles" basket for a neighbor during flu season.*

3/4 lb. boneless, skinless
   chicken strips
1/8 t. salt
1/8 t. pepper
1 T. oil
2 T. all-purpose flour

1/4 t. dried marjoram
14-oz. can chicken broth
1 c. water
1 onion, cut into wedges
1 c. green beans
1 c. carrots, peeled and shredded

Sprinkle chicken with salt and pepper. Heat oil in a large
saucepan over medium heat; add chicken and sauté until golden.
Sprinkle chicken with flour and marjoram; stir in broth, water and
vegetables. Bring soup to a boil; reduce heat, cover and simmer
for 5 minutes. Drop dumpling batter into hot soup by 1/4 cupfuls,
making 8 dumplings. Return soup to boiling. Reduce heat, cover
and simmer for 10 to 12 minutes, or until a toothpick inserted into a
dumpling comes out clean. Do not lift cover when simmering. Add
additional salt and pepper to taste, if desired. Makes 4 servings.

Dumplings:

2/3 c. biscuit baking mix
1/3 c. yellow cornmeal
1/4 to 1/2 c. shredded Cheddar
   cheese

1/2 c. milk

Stir together biscuit mix, cornmeal and cheese; stir in milk just
until moistened.

Soups & stews are so tasty served with warm bread.
Top each slice with the prettiest butter pats...simply use a
tiny cookie cutter to shape chilled butter slices.

COUNTRY-STYLE Soups & Breads

Winter Warm-Up Beef Simmer

Nancy Moore
Rochester, IN

*A thermos of this is just the thing for toting along on a
frosty hayride or football game. It's also ideal for warming
up little trick-or-treaters before they head outdoors.*

3 lbs. beef chuck, cut into
   2-inch cubes
6 slices bacon, cut into
   1/2-inch pieces
1 c. onion, chopped
8 redskin potatoes, halved
3 carrots, peeled and cut into
   1-inch pieces
8-oz. pkg. mushrooms, halved
3 onions, halved

1/2 c. fresh parsley, chopped
1 c. apple juice
10-1/2 oz. can beef broth
6-oz. can tomato paste
1/2 t. salt
1/2 t. pepper
1/2 t. dried thyme
1 t. garlic, minced
2 bay leaves

Cook beef, bacon and onion in a Dutch oven over medium-high heat
until browned, about 8 to 10 minutes, stir occasionally. Add remaining
ingredients; cover and bake at 325 degrees for 1-1/2 hours. Uncover
and bake for an additional 2 to 2-1/2 hours, stirring occasionally, until
beef is fork-tender. Remove and discard bay leaves. Serves 8.

A friend who's under-the-
weather will love it when you
deliver a goodie basket to her
door. Fill it with homemade
soup and bread, a good book
and pair of fuzzy slippers. Just
right for beating a winter cold!

Coffee Can Pumpkin Bread

Vickie

Surprise neighbors with this fragrant, moist bread. Give along with a crock of honey butter and a pretty vintage spreader.

4 eggs
3 c. sugar
2 15-oz. cans pumpkin
2/3 c. water
1 c. oil
2-1/2 c. all-purpose flour

2 t. baking soda
1/2 t. baking powder
1-1/2 t. salt
1 t. ground cloves
1 t. nutmeg
1 t. cinnamon

Beat eggs in a large mixing bowl; add sugar and mix well. Stir in pumpkin, water and oil; set aside. Combine remaining ingredients in another bowl and mix well; stir into egg mixture. Fill a greased one-pound coffee can 3/4 full. Bake at 325 degrees for 1-1/2 hours, or until top of bread springs to touch. When cool, run a knife around the edge to loosen and gently shake can upside-down to remove. Makes one loaf.

Sweet breads make
yummy lunchbox
sandwiches.
Top slices of pumpkin
or banana bread with
peanut butter, jam,
flavored cream cheese
or apple slices.
Kids will love 'em!

Pecan Pie Mini Muffins

Lisa Johnson
Hallsville, TX

Everyone's favorite pie made bite-size!

1 c. brown sugar, packed	2/3 c. butter, melted and cooled
1/2 c. all-purpose flour	2 eggs, beaten
1 c. chopped pecans	

Combine brown sugar, flour and pecans in a large bowl; set aside. In a medium bowl, stir together butter and eggs; mix well. Stir butter mixture into brown sugar mixture just until moistened. Fill greased and floured mini muffin cups 2/3 full. Bake at 350 degrees for 18 to 20 minutes, until muffins test done with a toothpick. Remove and cool on wire racks. Makes about 2-1/2 dozen.

Add unexpected Halloween greetings to your porch
with easy-to-make signs. Use acrylic paints
to decorate a plain length of wood with fun sayings.
Try something silly like "Free broom rides!"

Super-Simple Bread Bowls

Linda Behling
Cecil, PA

For larger bowls, halve the bread dough instead of cutting into thirds.

2 loaves frozen bread dough   2 eggs, beaten

Thaw bread according to package instructions; keep cold. Cut loaves into thirds; form each into a ball. Place on baking sheets sprayed with non-stick vegetable spray; brush with egg. Cover with plastic wrap sprayed with non-stick vegetable spray and let rise until double in bulk. Uncover; bake at 350 degrees for 25 minutes, or until golden. Cool. Slice off tops and hollow out bread. Makes 6 bowls.

Make a pumpkin cornucopia...a simple seasonal decoration.
Place a pumpkin on its flattest side, then hollow out the
rounded side. Fill the opening with apples, leaves,
bittersweet and rose hips. So simple, yet so pretty!

COUNTRY-STYLE
Soups & Breads

Easy as A, B, Seafood Bisque

Weda Mosellie
Phillipsburg, NJ

A big bowl of this soup is so good on chilly days.

6-oz. can crabmeat, drained
10-oz. pkg. imitation
   lobster, flaked
6-oz. can tiny shrimp, drained
1/2 c. butter plus 3 T. butter
1 onion, chopped
1 carrot, peeled and chopped
1 stalk celery, chopped

14-oz. can chicken broth
Optional: 1/2 c. white wine
1 T. tomato paste
3 c. half-and-half
1/2 c. flour
salt and pepper to taste
Garnish: fresh chives, chopped

Combine crabmeat, lobster and shrimp in a bowl; set aside. Melt
3 tablespoons butter in a large Dutch oven and sauté onion, carrot and
celery for about 3 minutes. Add chicken broth, seafood and wine, if
using. Bring to a boil; reduce heat and simmer. Stir in tomato paste
and half-and-half. Melt remaining butter and blend with flour in a
small bowl: stir into soup. Add salt and pepper to taste. Simmer over
low heat, stirring occasionally, for 40 minutes. Garnish with chives.
Serves 4 to 6.

A shimmery glass cake
stand is another easy-to-
make centerpiece. Just
stack apples of every
color on the stand and fill
in any openings with
russet and golden leaves.

Autumn Spice Bread

Judy Osborn
Pataskala, OH

Enjoy a loaf now, freeze the second to enjoy later.

3-1/2 c. all-purpose flour
2-1/2 c. sugar
2 t. baking soda
1-1/2 t. salt
1 t. cinnamon

1 t. nutmeg
2 c. canned pumpkin
1 c. corn oil
2/3 c. water
4 eggs

Stir together flour, sugar, baking soda, salt, cinnamon and nutmeg; set aside. In another bowl, mix pumpkin, oil and water; add eggs one at a time, beating well after each. Make a well in the center of the flour mixture; pour pumpkin mixture into well. Stir until thoroughly mixed; pour into 2 greased 9"x5" loaf pans. Bake at 350 degrees for one hour. Makes 2 loaves.

Soft Gingerbread

Holly Sutton
Grahamsville, NY

Oh-so yummy when warm slices are spread with whipped butter.

1/2 c. sugar
1 c. molasses
1/2 c. butter, softened
1 t. ground ginger
1 t. ground cloves

1 t. cinnamon
2 t. baking soda
1 c. boiling water
2-1/2 c. all-purpose flour
2 eggs, beaten

Mix all ingredients together; pour into a greased and floured 9"x5" loaf pan. Bake at 350 degrees for 35 to 40 minutes. Makes one loaf.

Raisin-Berry Bread

Sharon Gailey
Aston, PA

A scrumptious combination of flavors!

2 c. all-purpose flour
1 c. sugar
1-1/2 t. baking powder
1/2 t. baking soda
1 t. salt
1/4 c. margarine

1 egg, beaten
1 t. orange zest
3/4 c. orange juice
1-1/2 c. golden raisins
1-1/2 c. cranberries, chopped

Combine flour, sugar, baking power, baking soda and salt; cut in margarine until mixture is crumbly. Stir in egg, orange zest and orange juice until moist; fold in raisins and cranberries. Pour into a greased 9"x5" loaf pan; bake at 350 degrees for one hour and 10 minutes. Makes one loaf.

An old-fashioned wire egg basket looks terrific filled with pumpkins of every shape and size! Set it by the back door where it can greet friends as they drop by.

White Bean, Pasta & Sausage Soup

Cora Baker
Marion, OH

So savory...one bowl won't be enough!

1/2 lb. spicy ground Italian
   sausage
1 onion, chopped
3 cloves garlic, chopped
1 carrot, peeled and chopped
1-1/2 c. dried Great
   Northern beans
2 T. currants

6 c. chicken broth
3 c. water
1 t. dried basil
14-1/2 oz. can roma tomatoes
1 c. small shell pasta, uncooked
Garnish: grated Parmesan
   cheese

Place sausage, onion, garlic and carrot in a large saucepan over medium heat. Sauté until sausage is browned and vegetables are tender; drain. Stir in beans, currants, broth, water and basil; bring to a boil. Reduce heat and simmer for about 2-1/2 hours, or until beans are tender. Add tomatoes and pasta; simmer until pasta is tender, about 8 to 10 minutes. Sprinkle with cheese. Serves 4 to 6.

Spanish Rice Soup

Rebekah Anne Ptacnik
Ottawa, KS

A spicy soup that will warm you inside and out.

1 lb. ground beef, browned
   and drained
4 c. water
4 c. tomatoes, chopped
1 c. celery, chopped
1/4 c. green pepper, chopped
1/4 c. onion, chopped

1/2 c. instant rice, uncooked
1-1/2 oz. pkg. onion soup mix
1 T. beef bouillon granules
1/2 t. salt
1/2 t. dried basil
1/8 t. hot pepper sauce

Combine all ingredients in a large saucepan. Simmer over low heat for about 30 minutes. Makes 4 to 6 servings.

Rosemary Crisp Bread

Sharon Tillman
Hampton, VA

Try cutting into cubes and tossing on top of warm soup.

10-oz. tube refrigerated pizza
  dough
2 T. Dijon mustard
1 T. garlic, minced
2 t. olive oil

1-1/2 c. shredded Cheddar &
  mozzarella pizza-blend
  cheese
1 t. dried rosemary

Roll out pizza dough on a lightly greased jelly-roll pan. Pat out with fingers to a 12"x10" rectangle. Bake at 425 degrees for 5 minutes. Mix together mustard, garlic and oil; spread evenly over baked crust. Sprinkle with cheese and rosemary. Bake an additional 8 to 9 minutes, until cheese melts and crust is golden. Serves 10.

Use a hot glue gun to attach dried Chinese lantern flowers to a length of grapevine garland. Their blazing orange color looks beautiful draped around a doorway or along a porch railing.

Fiesta Cornbread

Kathryn Harris
Lufkin, TX

*If you'd like, shred Pepper-Jack cheese and substitute
for the Cheddar...it will add more kick!*

1 c. cornmeal
1 c. buttermilk
8-oz. can creamed corn
2 jalapeños, chopped
1/2 t. salt
3/4 t. baking soda

2 eggs, beaten
1 onion, chopped
1/4 c. oil
1 c. shredded mild Cheddar
    cheese, divided

Combine first 8 ingredients; set aside. Heat oil in an 8 to 10-inch cast
iron skillet; pour in half the batter. Sprinkle with half the cheese; pour
remaining batter over top. Sprinkle with remaining cheese; bake at
400 degrees for 30 minutes. Serves 6 to 9.

Trick-or-treaters will be tickled
to follow a twinkling path to get
their candy. String orange fairy
lights on bare tree branches,
then insert the branches into a
pumpkin for support. Set
several pumpkins along each
side of your sidewalk or path.

Chicken Fajita Chowder

Kelly Jones
Tallahassee, FL

*This takes a bit of time to prepare, but it's well worth it.
You'll have a savory soup that will be a new family favorite.*

3 T. all-purpose flour
1.4-oz. pkg. fajita or taco
   seasoning mix, divided
4 boneless, skinless chicken
   breasts, cubed
3 T. oil
1 onion, chopped
1 t. garlic, minced
15-1/4 oz. can sweet corn &
   diced peppers, drained
15-oz. can black beans,
   drained and rinsed
14-1/2 oz. can Mexican-style
   stewed tomatoes

4-1/2 oz. can chopped
   green chiles
3 c. water
1 c. instant brown
   rice, uncooked
Optional: dried cilantro to taste
10-3/4 oz. can nacho
   cheese soup
Garnish: sour cream, shredded
   Cheddar cheese, chopped
   green onions, crushed
   tortilla chips

Combine flour and 2 tablespoons seasoning mix in a large plastic zipping bag; add chicken. Seal bag and shake to coat. Sauté chicken in oil in a large Dutch oven over high heat, stirring often, about 5 minutes or until golden. Reduce heat to medium-high. Add onion and garlic; sauté for 5 minutes. Stir in remaining seasoning mix and all ingredients except soup and garnish. Bring to a boil; reduce heat to medium-low, cover and simmer for 5 minutes. Add soup; stir until heated through. Garnish as desired. Makes 8 to 10 servings.

When serving soups and stews, stack 2 or 3 cake stands, then fill each tier with a different type of roll for guests to try.

Smokey Hollow Vegetable Soup

Kathy Matthews
Sanford, NC

A favorite at our house and at our church...it tastes even better the next day!

1 lb. ground beef
1 onion, diced
28-oz. can crushed tomatoes
5 potatoes, peeled and cubed
2 15-oz. cans mixed
   vegetables, drained
15-1/4 oz. can corn, drained

14-1/2 oz. can lima beans,
   drained and rinsed
4-1/2 c. water
salt and pepper to taste
14-3/4 oz. can creamed corn
1-1/2 oz. pkg. onion soup mix

Brown meat and onion together in a large soup pot; drain. Add tomatoes, potatoes, mixed vegetables, corn, water, salt and pepper. Bring to a boil over medium heat. Reduce heat; simmer over very low heat for 2 hours. Add creamed corn and soup mix; simmer for an additional 30 minutes. Drop flattened tablespoonfuls of dumpling batter into soup. If needed add more hot water. When dumplings float to the top, turn over and continue cooking for a few more minutes. Makes 10 to 12 servings.

Corn Dumplings:

1 c. yellow cornmeal
1/4 c. self-rising flour

1/4 t. salt
1/2 c. water

Stir cornmeal, flour and salt together. Add just enough water to make a stiff batter.

Delicious autumn!
-George Eliot

Mini Pumpkin Loaves

*Connie Herek
Bay City, MI*

*The first year my husband and I were married, I made this recipe
for family & friends. Seven years later it has become
a much-requested favorite!*

3 c. all-purpose flour
1 T. plus 1 t. pumpkin
    pie spice
2 t. baking soda
1-1/2 t. salt
1 c. canned pumpkin

3 c. sugar
4 eggs
1 c. oil
1/2 c. orange juice
1 c. sweetened, dried cranberries

Combine flour, spice, baking soda and salt in a large bowl; set aside.
Combine pumpkin, sugar, eggs, oil and juice in a small bowl; beat just
until blended with an electric mixer on low speed. Add pumpkin
mixture to flour mixture; stir just until moistened. Fold in cranberries.
Spoon batter into six, greased and floured 5"x3" disposable loaf pans.
Bake at 350 degrees for 50 to 55 minutes, until a toothpick inserted in
center tests clean. Cool in pans for 10 minutes; remove to wire racks to
finish cooling. Makes 6 small loaves.

It's easy to personalize a lunchbox to make it one-of-a-kind.
Scan a favorite toy, doll or photo and print out on clear or
white water-resistant labels for ink-jet printers. Trim around
the edges and place on a metal or plastic lunchbox. Easy to
wipe clean and sure to be a hit!

Smoked Sausage Potato Soup

Hazel Kyzar
Glendale, AZ

The flavors combine to make a delicious, comforting bowl of soup.

6-oz. pkg. smoked sausage
   links, thinly sliced
3-1/2 oz. pkg. pepperoni slices
2 onions, chopped
2 10-3/4 oz. cans cream of
   celery soup

10-3/4 oz. can cream of
   chicken soup
2-1/2 c. milk
1-1/4 c. water
5 c. potatoes, peeled, cubed
   and cooked

Sauté sausage, pepperoni and onions in a large saucepan over medium heat until onions are golden. Drain; stir in remaining ingredients. Reduce heat and simmer without boiling for 15 minutes. Serves 8 to 10.

Serve up savory soups with leaf-shaped toast created by simply using a cookie cutter on toast slices.

COUNTRY-STYLE
Soups & Breads

Curried Pumpkin Soup

Carol Allston-Stiles
Newark, DE

This soup freezes well...just add the cream after thawing.

16-oz. pkg. sliced mushrooms
1/2 c. onion, chopped
2 T. butter
2 T. all-purpose flour
1 T. curry powder
3 c. chicken or vegetable broth
15-oz. can pumpkin

1 T. honey
1/8 t. nutmeg
salt and pepper to taste
1 c. whipping cream or
   evaporated milk
Garnish: sour cream, croutons

Sauté mushrooms and onion with butter in a large saucepan over medium heat until softened. Add flour and curry powder; cook over medium heat for 5 minutes, stirring constantly. Add broth, pumpkin, honey, nutmeg, salt and pepper to taste. Simmer for 15 minutes, stirring occasionally. Stir in cream or milk; heat through without boiling. Serve with a dollop of sour cream and croutons. Serves 6.

Sprucing up before the family visits? Everything old
is new again...freshen up walls with a coat of
old-fashioned whitewash paint!

Prize-Winning Chili

Debbie Joramo
Sleepy Eye, MN

This recipe is so good I won a prize for it! Full of flavor,
it's best served with thick slices of buttered cornbread.

2 T. oil
2 c. onion, chopped
salt and cayenne pepper to taste
2 lbs. stew beef, cubed
3 T. chili powder
1 T. ground cumin
1/4 t. red pepper flakes
1 T. dried oregano
2 T. garlic, chopped
3 c. crushed tomatoes
1/4 c. tomato paste

2 c. beef broth
1 c. canned dark red kidney
   beans, drained and rinsed
2 T. all-purpose flour
1/4 c. water
13-1/2 oz. pkg. tortilla chips
1-1/2 c. shredded Monterey
   Jack cheese
1/2 c. sour cream
6-oz. jar jalapeños, drained
   and chopped

Heat oil in a large saucepan over medium heat. Add onion and sauté
for 3 to 5 minutes, until tender. Sprinkle with salt and cayenne pepper
to taste. Stir in stew beef and spices; cook until meat is browned,
5 to 6 minutes. Stir in garlic, tomatoes, tomato paste, broth and beans;
bring to a boil. Reduce heat and simmer, uncovered, for one hour until
beef is tender, stirring occasionally. Skim off any fat. Mix flour and
water; slowly stir into chili. Simmer for an additional 30 minutes,
stirring occasionally. Add more salt and cayenne pepper, if desired.
To serve, place a handful of tortilla chips in each shallow bowl and
spoon chili over top. Garnish with shredded cheese, a dollop of sour
cream and a sprinkle of jalapeños. Serves 8 to 10.

Use a pumpkin or ghost-shaped cookie cutter to cut the center
from a slice of cheese. After spooning soup into bowls, top
servings with the cut-out shape or the cheese slice. How fun!

Corny Cornbread

Tina Stidam
Delaware, OH

A "must-have" whenever there's a gathering!

1 c. cornmeal
1 c. all-purpose flour
1/4 c. sugar
1 T. baking powder
1 t. salt

2 eggs, beaten
12-oz. can corn, drained
1-1/4 c. milk
1/4 c. oil

Mix together cornmeal, flour, sugar, baking powder and salt; set aside.
Stir together eggs, corn, milk and oil; add to flour mixture. Spoon into
a greased and floured 8"x8" baking pan; bake at 425 degrees for
30 to 35 minutes. Serves 9 to 12.

Show off pretty bedding and quilts in the linen closet.
Remove the door and replace it with an old-fashioned,
wooden screen door.

Halloween Soup

Bonnie Siatkowski
Mishawaka, IN

Here in Indiana, it is always cold and damp on Halloween.
Before my 3 daughters went out to trick or treat, they always had
this soup. Now that they're grown up, my granddaughter enjoys it.

5 c. water
8-oz. can tomato sauce
1-lb. pkg. hot dogs, sliced
1 c. elbow macaroni, uncooked

10-oz. pkg. frozen peas &
   carrots
1-1/2 oz. pkg. onion soup mix

Combine all ingredients in a saucepan; bring to a boil. Reduce heat;
cover and simmer for 10 minutes, or until macaroni is tender, stirring
occasionally. Makes 4 servings.

Bacon-Cheese Muffins

Debi DeVore
Dover, OH

So scrumptious topped with real butter.

1-1/2 c. all-purpose flour
1/2 c. cornmeal
1 T. baking powder
1/4 t. cayenne pepper
1/4 t. salt
2-1/3 c. shredded Cheddar
   cheese, divided

8 slices bacon, crisply
   cooked and crumbled
1 egg, beaten
1 c. milk
1/4 c. butter, melted

Combine flour, cornmeal, baking powder, cayenne pepper and salt in a
large bowl. Stir in 2 cups cheese and bacon; set aside. Blend together
egg, milk and butter in a medium bowl; stir into flour mixture just until
moistened. Fill greased muffin cups 3/4 full; sprinkle with remaining
cheese. Bake at 425 degrees for 12 to 15 minutes, until a toothpick
comes out clean. Let cool 5 minutes; remove from pan and cool on
wire rack. Serve warm. Makes one dozen.

COUNTRY-STYLE
Soups & Breads

Sour Cream Biscuits

Beverly Mock
Pensacola, FL

With only 3 ingredients, these biscuits are a dream to make any time.

1 c. butter, softened
8-oz. container sour cream

2 c. self-rising flour

Combine butter and sour cream; fold in flour. Fill greased muffin cups 3/4 full; bake at 400 degrees for 8 to 10 minutes, or until golden. Makes 2 dozen.

Broccoli-Cheese Soup

Janice Barnes
New Paris, OH

If you use the Mexican-style cheese spread, you'll give this soup a whole new taste!

3/4 c. onion, chopped
2 T. oil
6 c. water
6 cubes chicken bouillon
8-oz. pkg. thin egg noodles, uncooked
2 10-oz. pkgs. frozen chopped broccoli

6 c. milk
16-oz. pkg. pasteurized process cheese spread, diced
1 t. salt
1/8 t. pepper
1/8 t. garlic powder

Sauté onion in oil in a skillet over medium heat; set aside. Bring water to a boil in a stockpot; add bouillon, noodles and broccoli. Simmer until tender, about 7 to 10 minutes. Add remaining ingredients; reduce heat. Cover and simmer without boiling, until heated through. Makes 10 to 12 servings.

Take an autumn bike ride...fill the bike's basket with a thermos of soup and loaf of bread. What fun!

Patchwork Muffins

Toni Currin
Dillon, SC

A little of this, a little of that and you have the most tasty muffins!

2 c. all-purpose flour
3/4 c. sweetened,
   dried cranberries
1 t. baking powder
1/2 t. baking soda
1/2 t. cinnamon
1/2 t. ground cloves
1/4 t. nutmeg
1/4 t. salt
2 c. water

3/4 c. whipping cream
1/2 c. milk
2 eggs, beaten
1/2 c. brown sugar, packed
1/2 t. vanilla extract
1 c. canned pumpkin
1/4 c. butter, melted
1-1/4 c. semi-sweet
   chocolate chips

Mix together flour, cranberries, baking powder, baking soda, spices and salt; set aside. Stir together remaining ingredients except chocolate chips; blend with flour mixture. Spoon into greased muffin cups filling 2/3 full; bake at 375 degrees for 15 to 18 minutes. Place chocolate chips in a plastic zipping bag; microwave on high setting until chocolate is melted, stirring every 15 seconds. Snip a small corner off bag; drizzle over muffins. Makes one dozen.

Fill a basket or vintage lunchbox with muffins and deliver to a busy mom. She'll love the surprise and will have a sweet & simple after-school treat for the kids.

COUNTRY-STYLE
Soups & Breads

Butterscotch Bread

Mari Courtney
Lewisville, TX

Toss in some sweetened, dried cranberries if you'd like...you just can't go wrong with this recipe!

4 c. all-purpose flour
1-1/2 t. baking powder
1 t. baking soda
1/2 t. salt
2 c. brown sugar, packed

2 c. buttermilk
2 eggs
3 T. butter, melted
1 c. golden raisins
1 c. chopped pecans

Combine first 8 ingredients; beat with an electric mixer at low speed for 2 to 3 minutes. Stir in raisins and pecans; spoon into 2 greased 9"x5" loaf pans. Bake at 350 degrees for 40 to 50 minutes. Let stand in pans for 10 minutes; remove from pans to cool completely. Makes 2 loaves.

Serve up breads, muffins and rolls on a small flea-market-find doll bed...ideal as a whimsical serving tray!

Old-Fashioned Split Pea Soup

Judy Voster
Neenah, WI

*I created this recipe to suit my own taste...the bacon
and chicken broth make it special.*

16-oz. pkg. dried split peas
4 c. water, divided
6 c. chicken broth
1/2 lb. bacon, chopped
1/2 to 1-lb. meaty ham bone
3 to 4 carrots, peeled and
    chopped

2 stalks celery, sliced
2 onions, diced
1 t. salt
1 T. fresh parsley, chopped
1 t. dried chives

Combine peas and 2 cups water in a large stockpot; boil for
2 minutes. Remove from heat; cover and let stand for one hour to
overnight. Drain; add remaining water and ingredients except parsley
and chives. Bring to a boil and simmer over low heat for 2 hours.
Remove ham bone; cool and remove meat from bone. Add meat to
soup, discarding bone. Add herbs and simmer an additional hour.
Serves 8 to 10.

And at no season...do we get such superb color effects
as from August to November.

-Rose G. Kingsley

Slowly-Simmered Flavors of FALL

Hot Spicy Cider for a Crowd

Edith Bolstad
Beaver Dam, WI

A kit & kaboodle of spiced cider to sip...your secret to keeping warm on blustery days!

1 gal. apple cider
1 c. sugar
2 t. ground cloves

2 t. allspice
2 4-inch cinnamon sticks
1/4 c. orange juice

Combine all ingredients in a slow cooker. Cover and cook on low setting for 5 to 6 hours, or on high setting for 2 to 3 hours. Discard cinnamon sticks. Makes about 16 cups.

Hot Caramel Apple Cider

Kimberly Boyce
Murrieta, CA

Put it on before going out for a fall hayride or an afternoon of apple picking...the aroma will fill the whole house!

1/2 gal. apple cider
1/2 c. brown sugar, packed
1-1/2 t. cider vinegar
1 t. vanilla extract
1 4-inch cinnamon stick

6 whole cloves
1 orange, sliced
Optional: 1/2 c. apple jack liquor
Garnish: 1/3 c. caramel
    ice cream topping

Combine all ingredients except topping in a slow cooker. Cover; cook on low setting for 5 to 6 hours. Strain; discard spices and orange. Serve in mugs, drizzling a teaspoonful of topping into each mug. Serves 16.

The beauty that shimmers in
the yellow afternoons
of October, who could ever
clutch it?

-Ralph Waldo Emerson

Chai Tea

Linda Behling
Cecil, PA

Typically a sweet tea...reduce the sugar even more if you'd like.

8 c. water
8 teabags
1/2 to 3/4 c. sugar
16 whole cloves
5 4-inch cinnamon sticks
8 1-inch slices fresh ginger,
    peeled

Optional: 16 whole cardamom,
    seeds removed and pods
    discarded
1 c. milk

Combine all ingredients except milk in a slow cooker. Cover; cook on high setting for 2 to 2-1/2 hours. Strain and discard spices. Cover and refrigerate for up to 3 days, or serve immediately. Stir in milk just before serving. May be served warm or chilled. Serves 8 to 10.

Long, slender sticks are ideal for holding apples to be roasted at a bonfire...roll apples in cinnamon-sugar after roasting.
Yum!

Warm & Cozy Oatmeal

Laurie Wilson
Fort Wayne, IN

Wake up to the flavor of apples and brown sugar.

2 c. milk
1 c. quick-cooking
   oats, uncooked
1/4 c. brown sugar,
   packed
1 T. butter, melted

2 T. maple syrup
1 t. cinnamon
1 c. apple, cored, peeled
   and finely chopped
1/2 c. raisins
1/2 c. chopped walnuts

Combine all ingredients in a slow cooker sprayed with non-stick vegetable spray. Cover and cook on low setting for 7 to 8 hours. Stir before serving. Serves 6 to 8.

Breakfast Apple Cobbler

Bev Westfall
Berlin, NY

A favorite dessert now becomes an early-morning treat!

8 apples, cored,
   peeled and sliced
1/4 c. sugar
1/8 t. cinnamon

juice of 1 lemon
1/4 c. butter, melted
2 c. granola

Combine all ingredients in a slow cooker. Cover; cook on low setting for 7 to 9 hours, or on high setting for 2 to 3 hours. Serves 6 to 8.

Springy metal lawn chairs from the 1950's make for comfortable seating outside on a crisp fall day or around a cozy campfire at night.

Crunchy Coconut Granola

Sharon Demers
Dolores, CO

Add raisins, dried fruit, nuts or whatever your family likes best.

5 c. long-cooking oats,
   uncooked
1/2 c. oil
1/2 c. honey
1 t. vanilla extract

1 t. cinnamon
1 c. sweetened flaked
   coconut
1/8 t. salt

Mix all ingredients together and place in a slow cooker sprayed with non-stick vegetable spray. Cover, leaving lid slightly ajar, and cook on low setting for 5 hours, or until golden. Stir occasionally. Serves 6.

Cheesy Breakfast Casserole

Ellie Brandel
Clackamas, OR

I love this...it bakes while I sleep and is ready
in the morning to serve hungry family or overnight guests!

1/2 lb. ground pork sausage
mustard to taste
10 slices bread
8-oz. pkg. shredded sharp
   Cheddar cheese

6 eggs
1-1/2 c. milk
salt and pepper to taste

Cover sausage with water in a skillet; boil for 5 minutes. Drain. Brown and crumble sausage; drain and set aside. Spread mustard on one side of bread; cut each slice into 9 pieces. Layer bread, cheese and sausage in a slow cooker sprayed with non-stick vegetable spray. Beat together eggs, milk, salt and pepper; pour over casserole. Cover and cook on low setting for 8 to 12 hours. Serves 8.

Glazed Cocktail Sausages

Janice Dorsey
San Antonio, TX

*Put these savory sausages on to cook the morning of the
big football game...ready by game time!*

2 16-oz. pkgs. cocktail
   sausages
1 c. apricot preserves

1/2 c. maple syrup
2 T. bourbon or 1 to
   2 t. vanilla extract

Combine all ingredients in a slow cooker. Cover and cook on low
setting for 4 hours. Makes 16 to 20 servings.

Oniony Crab Dip

Lisa Colombo
Appleton, WI

This couldn't be easier to whip up...keep it warm in a slow cooker.

2 8-oz. pkgs. cream cheese
3 T. butter
1 bunch green onions, chopped

1 lb. crabmeat
onion and garlic salt to taste
crackers and garlic toast

Mix all ingredients together except crackers and toast in a microwave-
safe bowl. Microwave on high setting until warm. Pour into a slow
cooker; cover and keep warm on low setting. Serve with crackers and
garlic toast. Serves 24.

Tote your slow-cooker
appetizers to the game day
tailgating party. Keep hot
foods hot by picking up a
power inverter that will use
your car battery to power
appliances!

SLOWLY-SIMMERED
Flavors of Fall

Taco Joe Dip

Margie Beadles
Ozark, MO

Delicious, not too spicy and so easy to prepare.

16-oz. can kidney beans,
   drained and rinsed
15-1/4 oz. can corn, drained
15-oz. can black beans, drained
   and rinsed
14-1/2 oz. can stewed tomatoes

8-oz. can tomato sauce
4-oz. can chopped green chiles
1-1/4 oz. pkg. taco
   seasoning mix
1/2 c. onion, chopped
tortilla chips

Combine all ingredients except tortilla chips in a slow cooker. Cover and cook on low setting for 5 to 7 hours. Serve with tortilla chips. Makes 7 cups.

Pizza Fondue

Shannon Finewood
Corpus Christi, TX

Pepperoni chunks, mushrooms and other cut veggies
are good for dipping too.

28-oz. jar spaghetti sauce
16-oz. pkg. shredded mozzarella
   cheese
1/4 c. grated Parmesan cheese
2 T. dried oregano

2 T. dried parsley
1 T. garlic powder
1 t. dried, minced onion
1 loaf Italian bread, cut into
   bite-size cubes

Combine all ingredients except bread in a slow cooker; mix well. Cover and heat on low setting for 2 hours, until warmed through and cheese is melted; stir. Serve with bread for dipping. Makes 10 servings.

Swift autumn, like a bonfire of leaves.

-Elinor Wylie

Deliciously Cheesy Potatoes

Cathy Jepson
Salida, CA

This recipe has been in our family for many years. It's always requested by our children when we get together.

32-oz. pkg. frozen southern-
   style hashbrowns, thawed
2 10-3/4 oz. cans Cheddar
   cheese soup

2 12-oz. cans evaporated milk
2 2.8-oz. cans French fried
   onions, divided

Combine all ingredients except onions in a large bowl. Place half of mixture in a slow cooker; top with one can of onions. Place remaining potato mixture over onions; top with remaining can of onions. Cover; cook on low setting for 8 hours, stirring occasionally. Serves 8 to 10.

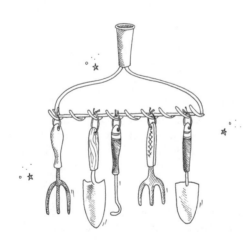

Fall means yard and garden clean-up. For a touch of whimsy, keep small gardening tools close at hand with the help of an old metal rake head. Mount it upside-down on the wall of a potting shed or garage.

Nutty Sweet Potatoes

Dianne Gregory
Conroe, TX

This will be a new favorite at the Thanksgiving dinner buffet!

2 lbs. sweet potatoes,
   peeled and grated
1/3 c. brown sugar, packed
1/4 c. margarine, melted
1/4 c. sweetened flaked coconut

1/4 c. chopped pecans, toasted
1/4 t. cinnamon
1/4 t. coconut flavoring
1/4 t. vanilla extract
Optional: toasted coconut

Combine sweet potatoes, brown sugar, margarine, coconut, pecans and cinnamon in a slow cooker. Cover and cook on low setting for 6 to 8 hours, or on high setting for 3 to 4 hours. Stir in coconut flavoring and vanilla. Sprinkle with toasted coconut, if desired. Makes 6 servings.

Bring a new twist to the classic Jack-'O-Lantern. Use a small drill bit to drill holes in any pattern into small gourds. Insert one or 2 bulbs from a string of tiny lights into each gourd, then arrange the lighted gourds in an urn. Surround them with fall leaves that will hide the electric cord.

Homestyle Cornbread Dressing

Tracy Chitwood
Van Buren, MO

Put this on the last couple hours the turkey is baking.

8-1/2 oz. pkg. cornbread mix
8 slices day-old bread, torn
4 eggs, beaten
1 onion, chopped
1/4 c. celery, chopped
2 10-3/4 oz. cans cream of
 chicken soup
2 14-1/2 oz. cans
 chicken broth
1-1/2 T. dried sage
1 t. salt
1/4 t. pepper
2 T. margarine, sliced

Prepare cornbread according to package directions; cool and crumble. Mix together all ingredients except margarine. Pour into a lightly greased slow cooker; dot with margarine. Cover and cook on low setting for 4 hours, or on high setting for 2 hours. Makes 16 servings.

Just for fun, slip a little note of encouragement into your child's lunchbox each week.

Saucy Red Beans

Lou Garraway
Saint Francisville, LA

So simple to make...it's a must at every gathering.

16-oz. pkg. dried red
   kidney beans
8 c. water, divided
1 onion, coarsely chopped
16-oz. can diced tomatoes
2 cloves garlic, minced

1 t. red pepper flakes
2 t. salt
Optional: 1/4 lb. salt pork
   or bacon, chopped
2 t. ground cumin
prepared rice

Cover beans with 4 cups water in a large pot. Let stand overnight; drain. Combine beans with remaining water and ingredients except rice in a slow cooker; stir well. Cover and cook on high setting for 2 hours; reduce to low setting and cook for an additional 8 hours. Serve over cooked rice. Serves 6.

Roasted pumpkin seeds are so delicious! Rinse 2 cups of seeds; dry on paper towels. Toss with one tablespoon of oil and place on an ungreased baking sheet. Bake at 350 degrees for 20 minutes; stir every 5 minutes. Remove from oven and sprinkle with salt.

Northern Sausage Soup

*Shelly Warner
Jennings, FL*

The longer this soup simmers, the better it tastes! Anyone who might drop by gets a hot cup of soup to enjoy.

1-lb. pkg. smoked sausage, divided
2 16-oz. cans Great Northern beans, drained and rinsed

2 14-1/2 oz. cans beef broth
1 onion, chopped

Remove and coarsely chop 2 sausage links from package, reserving remaining sausage for another recipe. Stir-fry sausage over medium heat in a non-stick skillet for about 4 minutes, or until lightly browned. Place sausage and remaining ingredients in an ungreased slow cooker. Cover and cook on high setting for one hour. Turn down to low setting; cook for an additional 8 to 9 hours. Makes 4 servings.

A dandy placecard how-to...preserve dried leaves by ironing between 2 sheets of wax paper under a tea towel. When cool, trim around the leaves and write guests' names on with metallic ink.

146

Garlicky Chicken Stew

Jeff Reichert
Gooseberry Patch

Tell those Halloween "vampires" to shoo!

4 boneless, skinless chicken
   thighs
3-1/2 c. chicken broth
2 c. plum tomatoes, chopped
1 c. green pepper, chopped
1 c. onion, chopped
1/2 c. long-cooking rice,
   uncooked

1/2 c. garbanzo beans, drained
   and rinsed
3 cloves garlic, chopped
1/2 t. salt
1/2 t. pepper
1 bay leaf
garnish: shredded Monterey Jack
   cheese, diced avocado

Combine all ingredients except cheese and avocado in a slow cooker.
Cover; cook on low setting for 7 to 9 hours, until chicken and rice are
tender. Remove and discard bay leaf. To serve, place a chicken thigh in
each soup bowl; top with soup and garnish as desired. Serves 4.

There are lots of beautiful flowers that like the
chilly autumn nights. Fill urns and windowboxes
with mums, pansies or decorative cabbages.

Autumn Supper Chicken

Debbie Byrne
Clinton, CT

*With just a few ingredients, this is ready for the slow cooker
in no time...go jump in the fall leaves!*

4 boneless, skinless chicken
   breasts
1-1/4 oz. pkg. taco seasoning
   mix

1 c. salsa
1/4 c. sour cream
tortillas or rice

Place chicken breasts in a lightly greased slow cooker; sprinkle
seasoning mix over chicken. Top with salsa; cover and cook on low
setting for 8 hours. Remove chicken to a plate; shred and set aside.
Add sour cream to salsa mixture; stir in chicken. Serve with tortillas
or over rice. Serves 4.

A sunny fall Saturday is the perfect time to host a bulb
planting party under the trees. Load a farm table with terra
cotta pots, trowels and spring-blooming bulbs. Fill galvanized
tubs or sap buckets with potting soil, then get digging!
Everyone goes home with potted daffodils and tulips along
with a cheery anticipation of what's to come.

Farmhouse Pork & Sauerkraut

Diane Cohen
Kennesaw, GA

This dish really warms you up on those chilly days.
The apple and potato disappear into the cheese soup
as they cook, making a delicious sauce.

4-lb. pork loin roast
1 T. oil
29-oz. can sauerkraut, drained
   and rinsed
1/4 c. water
1 onion, sliced
1 potato, peeled and sliced

10-3/4 oz. can Cheddar
   cheese soup
1 T. caraway seed
1 Granny Smith apple, cored,
   peeled and sliced
salt and pepper to taste

In a skillet over medium heat, brown pork in oil on all sides; place in
a slow cooker. Combine remaining ingredients except salt and pepper
in a large bowl. Pour over roast; cover and cook on low setting for
10 hours. Season with salt and pepper before serving. Serves 6.

Autumn flea market trips are a must! The weather is cool and
driving down a long country lane is a simple pleasure all by
itself. Pack all those goodies in every nook & cranny in your
pickup. It's amazing how many things will fit under a car seat!

Bacon-Corn Chowder

Linda Keehn
Chatham, IL

Ideal for toting to a harvest bonfire supper.

5 c. redskin potatoes, cubed
16-oz. pkg. frozen corn
6 slices bacon, crisply cooked
   and crumbled
1/4 c. dried, minced onion
2 14-1/2 oz. cans chicken broth
1 c. water

2 t. garlic salt
1 t. pepper
1/4 t. turmeric
12-oz. can evaporated milk
8-oz. pkg. shredded Monterey
   Jack cheese
Optional: fresh chives, chopped

Combine all ingredients except milk, cheese and chives in a slow cooker. Cover; cook on low setting for 8 to 9 hours, or until potatoes are tender. Stir in milk and cheese; cover until cheese melts. Garnish with chives, if desired. Makes 4 to 6 servings.

Country-Style Ham Au Gratin

Joshua Logan
Corpus Christi, TX

Ham and cheese just seem to go together and
never better than in this creamy dish.

2 c. cooked ham, diced
2 c. milk
1 c. boiling water
10-3/4 oz. can Cheddar cheese
   soup

7.8-oz. pkg. cheesy scalloped
   potato mix
2 11-oz. cans sweet corn &
   diced peppers, drained

Combine all ingredients in a slow cooker; mix well. Cover and cook on low setting for 8 to 9 hours. Makes 4 to 6 servings.

Indian Summer Rice

Kathie Williams
Oakland City, IN

Swap out the spinach for frozen broccoli if you'd like.

1 c. onion, chopped
1 c. celery, chopped
1 c. margarine
2 10-oz. pkgs. frozen chopped
  spinach, thawed and drained
2 10-3/4 oz. cans cream of
  mushroom soup

3 c. instant rice, uncooked
16-oz. jar pasteurized process
  cheese sauce
8-oz. can sliced mushrooms,
  drained
1/2 c. warm water

Sauté onion and celery in margarine until tender; transfer to a bowl and stir in remaining ingredients. Mix well; spoon into a slow cooker. Cover and cook on high setting for 30 minutes. Reduce heat to low setting and cook for an additional 2 hours. Serves 8 to 10.

A rustic buffet table...set an old door on top of hay bales!

Farmers' Market Stew

Verona Haught
Londonderry, NH

Autumn means the last of the farmers' markets, so gather as many fresh fall veggies as you can for this hearty dish.

1/2 lb. stew beef, cut into
   1-inch cubes
2 1/2-inch thick boneless
   pork chops, cubed
1 T. olive oil
2 carrots, peeled and chopped
2 parsnips, peeled and chopped
2 potatoes, peeled and chopped
1 stalk celery, chopped
2 apples, cored, peeled and
   cut into 1-inch cubes

2 T. quick-cooking tapioca,
   uncooked
1 c. apple cider
1 c. water
2 t. beef bouillon granules
Optional: 1/2 c. red wine
1/4 t. pepper
1/4 t. dried thyme
1/4 t. dried rosemary
salt to taste

Brown beef and pork in oil in a large skillet over medium heat; drain. Place vegetables and apples in a slow cooker; sprinkle with tapioca. Add beef and pork. Combine remaining ingredients in a small bowl; pour over beef and pork. Cover and cook on low setting for 8 to 10 hours, or on high setting for 4 to 5 hours. Add salt to taste before serving. Makes 6 servings.

Make lunch fun...create veggie rockets for kids' lunchboxes!
Layer thinly sliced carrots and cucumbers on a
lollipop stick for the rocket body. Top off each stick
with a single baby corn.

Apple-Glazed Pork Roast

Jen Eveland-Kupp
Temple, PA

*This roast cooks up so moist! I serve it alongside
mashed potatoes and green beans.*

3 to 4-lb. pork loin roast
salt and pepper to taste
4 to 6 apples, cored and
    quartered

1/4 c. apple juice
3 T. brown sugar, packed
1 t. ground ginger

Rub roast with salt and pepper. Brown briefly under broiler to remove excess fat; drain well. Arrange apples in bottom of a slow cooker; place roast on top. Combine remaining ingredients and spoon over roast. Cover and cook on low setting for 10 to 12 hours. Serves 6.

Whimsical candlesticks...use a paring knife to carve
a hole in the center of mini pumpkins. Make it just big
enough so that a taper will sit snugly. Because the bottoms of
pumpkins aren't flat, place each pumpkin on
top of a candlestick so it will be level.

Dutch Spareribs & Dumplings

Sharon Crider
Lebanon, MO

Dumplings are stick-to-your-ribs fall fare!

3 lbs. country-style pork
    spareribs
29-oz. can sauerkraut, drained
    and rinsed
2 tart apples, cored, peeled
    and cut into wedges

1 c. onion, chopped
2 t. seasoned salt
1/2 t. seasoned pepper
1/4 t. caraway seed

Slice spareribs into serving portions and trim any excess fat; place in a lightly greased slow cooker. Top ribs with sauerkraut, apples and onion; sprinkle with seasonings. Cover and cook on low setting for 8 hours, or until ribs are very tender when pierced. Remove excess liquid above sauerkraut with a bulb baster. Drop dumplings by heaping tablespoonfuls on top of sauerkraut. Cover and cook on high setting for 30 minutes, or until dumplings are fluffy. Serves 4 to 6.

Dumplings:

2 c. all-purpose flour
2 t. baking powder
1 t. salt

1/2 t. caraway seed
1 egg
3/4 c. milk

Combine flour, baking powder and salt in a large bowl; stir in caraway seed. Beat egg in a cup with a fork; beat in milk. Pour all at once into flour mixture; stir until blended.

Chicken-Netti

Lynn Knepp
Montgomery, IN

The kids will love this...so will the grown-ups!

16-oz. pkg. spaghetti, prepared
2 c. chicken broth
10-3/4 oz. can cream of
  mushroom soup
10-3/4 oz. can cream of
  chicken soup
4 to 6 green onions, chopped

16-oz. pkg. pasteurized process
  cheese spread, cubed
4 boneless, skinless chicken
  breasts, cooked and cubed
1/8 t. celery salt
1/8 t. pepper

Combine all ingredients in a slow cooker. Cover and cook on low setting for 2 to 3 hours, stirring frequently, until warmed through. Serves 8 to 10.

Autumn is indeed the
crowning glory of the year.

-Rose G. Kingsley

Roasted Turkey Breast

Amy Dyer
Dowelltown, TN

I created this recipe and love it so much,
I never cook turkey any other way!

10-lb. turkey breast
margarine, softened
salt to taste

14-1/2 oz. can chicken broth
2 T. dried, minced onion

Rinse turkey breast and pat dry with paper towels. Rub turkey with margarine, or spray with butter-flavored non-stick vegetable spray. Sprinkle with salt. Place turkey in a slow cooker sprayed with non-stick vegetable spray; add broth and onion. Cover and cook on low setting for 7 hours, until turkey is very tender. Remove turkey from broth; discard skin and bones. If desired, broth may be strained and returned with sliced turkey to slow cooker on low setting to keep warm for serving. Serves 10 to 12.

When family comes to visit for a fall reunion, spruce up your home in fresh, unexpected ways. Vintage aprons easily become window valances, milk bottles are vases and ironstone bowls hold bathroom soaps and towels. You can even frame county fair ribbons for whimsical artwork!

Beef Paprika

Roxanne Pepper
West Franklin, NH

Loaded with flavor!

2 to 3 lbs. stew beef, cubed
2 T. oil
2 to 3 T. water
6-oz. can tomato paste
2 cloves garlic, chopped

1-1/2 T. paprika
1 t. salt
2 green peppers, sliced
8-oz. container sour cream

Brown beef in oil in a skillet over medium-high heat. Place in a lightly greased slow cooker; add water, tomato paste, garlic, paprika and salt. Cover; cook on low setting for about 8 hours. Stir in green peppers the last 10 minutes of cooking; add sour cream just before serving. Serves 6.

Italian-Style French Dip

Christine Schnaufer
Geneseo, IL

Don't forget to serve this with thick, crusty rolls.

4-lb. beef bottom roast
14-oz. can beef broth with
    onions
1 green pepper, sliced

1.05-oz. pkg. Italian salad
    dressing mix
8 buns, split

Place roast in a slow cooker; combine remaining ingredients and pour over top. Cover and cook on low setting for 8 to 10 hours. Let cool; slice roast thinly and return to juice. Serve on buns. Serves 8.

Time for treats and fun! Lead trick-or-treaters to your door with a painted sign that says "Fright this way."

Savory Low Country Shrimp & Grits

Sharon Candler
Villa Rica, GA

Paired with a fresh spinach salad, this is a favorite meal.

6 c. chicken broth
3/4 t. salt
1-1/2 c. quick-cooking grits,
　uncooked
1 green pepper, chopped
1/2 c. red pepper, chopped
6 green onions, chopped
2 cloves garlic, minced
1-1/2 lb. small shrimp, peeled
　and cleaned

2 T. butter
1-1/2 c. shredded sharp
　Cheddar cheese
1-1/2 c. shredded Monterey
　Jack cheese
2　10-oz. cans diced tomatoes
　with chiles, drained
Optional: 1/4 t. cayenne pepper

Place broth, salt and grits in a slow cooker; cover and cook on low setting for 6 to 8 hours. Two hours before serving, sauté peppers, onions, garlic and shrimp in butter until vegetables are tender and shrimp are pink. Add vegetable mixture to slow cooker along with cheeses, tomatoes and cayenne pepper, if using. Continue to cook on high setting for an additional 2 hours. Serves 4 to 6.

Fill a bicycle's wire basket to overflowing with treats for visiting ghosts and goblins. After Halloween, create a festive fall welcome with a basket full of pumpkins, gourds, bittersweet vines and fall leaves.

Italian Chicken

Nola Coons
Gooseberry Patch

*The spaghetti sauce mix is the secret flavoring to this
quick-to-fix slow-cooked dinner.*

1 t. garlic powder
1 t. seasoned salt
1 t. pepper
3 lbs. chicken, skin removed
1 T. oil
1-1/2 oz. pkg. spaghetti
   sauce mix

1-1/2 t. Italian seasoning
1 c. dry white wine or
   chicken broth
4 c. zucchini, sliced
   1/2-inch thick
Optional: prepared thin spaghetti

Mix garlic powder, seasoned salt and pepper in a cup; rub chicken with
mixture. Heat oil in a large skillet over medium heat; brown chicken
on all sides, about 2 minutes. Combine chicken, sauce mix, Italian
seasoning and wine or broth in a slow cooker. Cover and cook on low
setting for 7 to 8 hours, or high setting for 3 to 4 hours. Add zucchini
during last hour of cooking and cook on low setting. If desired, serve
over hot cooked spaghetti. Makes 6 servings.

For a super-simple table runner, knit squares of the same size
in different colors, then stitch together.

Nutty Chocolate Fudge

Patricia Barnett
Hillsboro, MO

My mom swears this is the best fudge she has ever tasted!

3 8-oz. pkgs. dark melting
   chocolate
4 6-oz. pkgs. white melting
   chocolate
4-oz. pkg. sweet baking
   chocolate, chopped

12-oz. pkg. semi-sweet
   chocolate chips
2 12-oz. jars salted peanuts

Place dark chocolate, white chocolate and sweet chocolate in a slow cooker; cover and cook on low setting until melted. Add chocolate chips and peanuts; continue to cook, covered, on low setting. Stir; cover and cook for an additional hour. Stir again and cook for an additional hour. Drop by tablespoonfuls onto wax paper; cool completely. Store in an airtight container for up to 3 months. Makes about 4 dozen pieces.

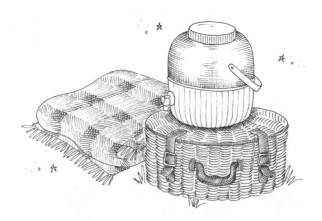

This year, tote a picnic to the pumpkin patch! Crisp air, blue skies and family...perfect for memory making.

Golden Peach Cobbler

Jennifer Vallimont
Kersey, PA

Spoon a little whipping cream on each serving for a yummy treat.

1/3 c. biscuit baking mix
2/3 c. quick-cooking oats,
   uncooked
1/2 c. brown sugar, packed

1 t. cinnamon
4 c. sliced peaches
1/2 c. peach juice or water
Optional: vanilla ice cream

Combine baking mix, oats, brown sugar and cinnamon in a slow cooker. Stir in peaches and juice or water. Cover and cook on low setting for 5 to 6 hours. If desired, remove lid for last 30 minutes to crisp the top. Serve with ice cream, if desired. Serves 4 to 6.

Tin cans with colorful, vintage-looking labels make the best country-style vases. Fill several with small bouquets of mums and march them along a windowsill or mantel.

Triple Chocolate Cake

Joan Brochu
Hardwick, VT

I also added some raspberries on top of the ice cream.

18-1/2 oz. pkg. chocolate
    cake mix
8-oz. container sour cream
3.9-oz. pkg. instant
    chocolate pudding mix

12-oz. pkg. chocolate chips
4 eggs, beaten
3/4 c. oil
1 c. water
Optional: vanilla ice cream

Place all ingredients except ice cream in a slow cooker; mix well. Cover and cook on high setting for 3 to 4 hours. If desired, serve with ice cream. Makes 8 to 10 servings.

Begin a new and heartfelt Thanksgiving tradition. Ask your friends & family to bring a pair of warm mittens or gloves to dinner, then deliver them to your local shelter.

A Thankful Heart...
Harvest
Main Dishes

Autumn Pork with Apple Chutney   *Jo Ann*

*Keeping the doctor away is delicious with this savory
fruit-filled apple dish!*

2 1-lb. pork tenderloins
1 clove garlic, minced
1 T. ground ginger
1 T. mustard seed

1 T. red pepper flakes
1 t. allspice
1 t. fennel seed
1 t. dried thyme

Rinse pork and pat dry with a paper towel. Place garlic and seasonings
in a blender; grind to a powder. Coat pork with powder. Place pork in
a lightly greased shallow roasting pan. Roast at 450 degrees for 20 to
25 minutes, or until juice is no longer pink when pierced. To serve,
slice pork into 1/2-inch medallions and top with chutney. Serve
remaining chutney on the side. Serves 6.

Chutney:

1 apple, cored, peeled
    and chopped
3/4 c. fennel, diced
3/4 c. brown sugar, packed
1/4 c. chopped pecans

1/3 c. raisins
1 T. crystallized ginger, chopped
1/2 t. salt
1/2 c. cider vinegar

Combine all ingredients in a medium saucepan; mix well. Bring to a boil.
Reduce heat to low; cover and cook 15 minutes. Remove cover and
cook an additional 15 to 20 minutes, or until fruit is tender; set aside.

Gather 'round the table for a Thanksgiving dinner that's
served potluck-style this year! Everyone brings what they're
famous for making or just their favorite dish. It's all about
celebrating food, family & friends.

Cranberry Pot Roast

Suellen Anderson
Rockford, IL

Sometimes I substitute a 2 to 3-pound tenderloin or brisket. Reduce the baking time to about one hour, or until a meat thermometer registers 125 to 130 degrees for medium-rare.

2 to 3-lb. pork or beef roast
1/2 c. sugar
salt and pepper to taste
1 T. butter

1/2 c. sherry vinegar
12-oz. pkg. cranberries
juice and zest of one orange

Dredge roast in sugar; reserve any remaining sugar. Sprinkle with salt and pepper; set aside. Melt butter in skillet over medium-high heat. Add roast and brown meat on all sides. Add vinegar; cook for one minute. Stir in cranberries and reserved sugar; mix in orange juice and zest. Reduce heat to low; cover and cook for about 2 hours, stirring every 30 minutes. Serves 4 to 6.

Whenever you prepare squash as a side dish for dinner, don't discard the seeds...they make delicious snacks when toasted. Scoop out the seeds; rinse, and pat dry. Lightly coat them with olive oil and season with coarse salt. Spread on an ungreased baking sheet and bake 12 to 15 minutes in a 350-degree oven. Toasted seeds will stay fresh up to 3 days in an airtight container.

Roast Turkey with Sage Butter

Kendall Hale
Lynn, MA

An All-American dish that's perfect for your harvest table.

1 c. butter, softened
3 T. fresh sage, chopped
8 slices bacon, crisply cooked
   and crumbled
salt and pepper to taste
16-lb. turkey, thawed if frozen

3 c. leeks, chopped
8 fresh sage sprigs
3 bay leaves, crumbled
4-1/3 c. chicken broth, divided
Garnish: fresh sage and
   parsley sprigs

Mix butter, sage and bacon in a medium bowl; sprinkle lightly with salt and pepper. Set aside. Remove giblets and neck from thawed turkey; reserve for another recipe. Rinse turkey and pat dry. Sprinkle inside of turkey with salt and pepper; add leeks, sage sprigs and bay leaves. Loosen skin and spread 1/3 cup butter mixture over breast meat under skin. Place turkey on a rack in a large ungreased roasting pan. Rub 2 tablespoons butter mixture on outside of turkey. Set aside 1/3 cup butter mixture for gravy; reserve remainder for basting. Pour 1/3 cup broth over turkey. Roast turkey at 350 degrees for about 3 hours, or until a meat thermometer inserted into thickest part of inner thigh registers 180 degrees. Baste turkey every 30 minutes with 1/3 cup broth; occasionally brush with remaining butter mixture. Transfer turkey to platter; keep warm. Let stand 30 minutes. To make gravy, pour pan juices and golden bits from roasting pan into large glass measuring cup. Spoon off fat; discard. Pour juices into a large saucepan over high heat. Add 2 cups broth. Boil until liquid is reduced to 2 cups, about 10 minutes. Whisk in reserved 1/3 cup butter mixture. Season with pepper. Garnish with sage and parsley. Serve turkey with gravy. Serves 12.

All seasons sweet, but autumn
best of all.

-Elinor Wylie

Sunday Chicken & Dressing

Laura Strausberger
Roswell, GA

This recipe is so easy and so good. With a combination like that, you just can't go wrong!

10-3/4 oz. can cream of
   chicken soup
10-3/4 oz. can cream of celery or
   cream of mushroom soup
1 c. chicken broth

2-1/2 to 3 lbs. cooked chicken,
   cubed
2 6-oz. pkgs. chicken-flavored
   stuffing mix, prepared

Combine soups and broth in a bowl; set aside. Place half of chicken in a lightly greased 13"x9" baking pan; top with half of stuffing and half of soup mixture. Repeat layers, ending with soup mixture. Bake at 350 degrees for one hour. Serves 12.

Create a centerpiece on-the-go! Fill an antique wire basket with a variety of pumpkin colors and sizes. Oh-so pretty on the table before dinner, then it's easily moved to the sideboard when dinner is served.

Praline Mustard-Glazed Ham

Sheri Dulaney
Englewood, OH

A beautiful ham served with a savory raisin sauce.

7 to 8-lb. bone-in, smoked
   spiral-cut ham half
1 c. maple syrup
3/4 c. brown sugar, packed
3/4 c. Dijon mustard

1/3 c. apple juice
1/4 c. raisins
1 tart apple, cored, peeled and
   thinly sliced

Remove and discard skin and any excess fat from ham. Place in a lightly greased 13"x9" baking pan; insert a meat thermometer in thickest part of ham. Combine syrup, brown sugar, mustard and apple juice; pour over ham. Set pan on lowest oven rack. Bake at 350 degrees, basting with drippings every 20 minutes for 2-1/2 hours, or until thermometer reads 140 degrees. Let ham stand for 10 minutes; remove from pan to a platter, reserving drippings. Use a bulb baster to remove and discard fat from drippings. To make sauce, heat drippings with raisins and apples in a small saucepan over low heat for 5 minutes. Serve sliced ham with warm sauce. Serves 12.

Did you know a vintage plant stand makes a terrific centerpiece? It's just the right size for holding silverware tucked inside terra cotta pots, a sugar bowl or even a selection of yummy pies!

A THANKFUL HEART ...
Harvest Main Dishes

New England Turkey & Stuffing

Amber Erskine
Hartland, VT

This stuffing was always a Thanksgiving tradition at our home...my dad would grind everything together in a hand-cranked meat grinder. Now I prepare it, and I wouldn't have it any other way!

2-1/2 loaves day-old bread, torn
    into 1-inch pieces
20-lb. turkey, thawed if frozen
1-1/2 lbs. ground pork sausage,
    browned and drained
2 eggs
2 c. canola oil

3 c. onion, minced
1/2 c. celery, diced
3 T. poultry seasoning
1-1/2 T. salt
1/2 t. pepper
1/2 cup melted butter

Place bread in a large bowl; set aside. Remove giblets and neck from thawed turkey; reserve neck for another recipe. Place giblets in a medium saucepan; add water to cover. Simmer gently over medium heat for 1-1/2 hours; drain. Place giblets and remaining ingredients except turkey and butter in a food processor or meat grinder. Process until finely chopped. Pour over bread; mix with hands until bread is coated. Set aside. Rinse turkey and pat dry with paper towels. Stuff turkey with bread mixture; place in a lightly greased roasting pan. Cover turkey with cheesecloth that has been soaked with melted butter. Roast for 12 to 14 minutes per pound at 450 degrees for first 30 minutes. Reduce heat to 350 degrees for remaining time; baste with melted butter every 30 minutes. Remove cheesecloth 30 minutes before turkey is done to allow browning. Serves 20 to 24.

Little ones love to help out in the kitchen, so tuck a set of measuring spoons, oven mitt and mini rolling pin in the pocket of a child-size apron...everything a little helper needs.

Martelli Pasta Gravy

Nichole Martelli
Alvin, TX

One of the first recipes that I learned to make after my husband and I married. It was always a favorite for his family and has now become one of my favorites as well.

1/2 c. butter
1/4 c. oil
3-lb. pork loin roast
6 to 8 onions, chopped
1 bunch celery, chopped
1 bunch fresh parsley, chopped
1 clove garlic, chopped
2 14-1/2 oz. cans diced
    tomatoes

2 29-oz. cans tomato sauce
2 18-oz. cans tomato paste
2 4-oz. cans mushrooms,
    drained
2 bay leaves
1 t. allspice
1 t. ground cloves
1 t. flavor enhancer

Heat butter and oil in a stockpot over medium heat; add roast and brown on all sides. Remove from stockpot and set aside. Stir in onions, celery, parsley and garlic; sauté until tender. Stir in diced tomatoes; cook for 15 to 20 minutes over low heat. Add remaining ingredients; stir to blend. Add pork and simmer, covered, over low heat for 6 to 8 hours. Remove and discard bay leaves. Serve over cooked pasta. Makes 10 to 12 servings.

Arrangements of autumn leaves and berries
make the best autumn greeting. Wire them to a simple
grapevine wreath or bunch together, secure with a rubber
band and top with a raffia bow. Either will create
a warm welcome on your front door.

Hearty Red Beans & Rice

Laurel Perry
Loganville, GA

*So filling, so fabulous, this tasty main dish is one
you'll want to prepare again and again.*

2 lbs. dried red kidney beans
7 slices bacon, sliced into
    2-inch pieces
2 lbs. Kielbasa, diced
1-1/2 c. cooked ham, diced
6 cloves garlic, minced
4 stalks celery, diced
2 green peppers, diced

2 onions, chopped
2 32-oz. cans chicken broth
2 c. water
salt and pepper to taste
seafood seasoning to taste
prepared rice

Cover beans with water in a bowl; let stand for 6 to 8 hours. Drain and
rinse well; set aside. Sauté bacon in a Dutch oven over medium-high
heat for 5 minutes. Add Kielbasa and ham; cook until browned. Add
garlic and vegetables; cook until tender. Stir in beans, broth, water and
seasonings; bring to a boil. Reduce heat and simmer for 3 hours, or
until beans are tender, stirring occasionally. Serve over cooked rice.
Makes 14 to 16 servings.

Make fall dinners fun for the kids
too with a clever table runner for
the kids' table. Sew a border of
bandanna print fabric all around
the runner edges. Remove the back
pockets from old jeans and stitch
them on each end. Fill pockets with
forks, straws and napkins!

Old-Fashioned Chicken Pot Pie

Donna Riggins
Albertville, AL

Makes 2 savory pies...share one with a neighbor.

4 frozen pie crusts, thawed
    and divided
5 to 6 boneless, skinless chicken
    breasts, cooked and chopped
1 onion, chopped
10-3/4 oz. can cream
    of chicken soup

10-3/4 oz. can cream of
    mushroom soup
8-oz. container sour cream
salt and pepper to taste

Line two 9" pie plates with one crust each; set aside. Combine remaining ingredients except remaining crusts in a large bowl; mix well. Divide between pie plates; top with remaining crusts. Crimp crusts to seal; cut several slits in top crusts. Bake at 350 degrees for 35 to 45 minutes, until bubbly and crusts are golden. Makes 2 pies, 6 servings each.

Create a simple fall decoration with no fuss. Use a tiered lazy Susan and layer on mini pumpkins, apples, leaves and berries.

Parmesan Pork Chop Bake

Chris Elston
Trabuco Canyon, CA

I serve this dish with roasted asparagus and a green salad...one of my family's favorite dinners.

1/2 c. butter, melted
2 to 3 t. garlic powder
2 c. Italian-seasoned dry bread
  crumbs

3/4 c. grated Parmesan cheese
4 to 6 boneless pork chops
salt and pepper to taste
1/4 c. olive oil

Mix butter and garlic powder in a large shallow bowl; set aside. Combine bread crumbs and cheese. Dip pork chops into butter mixture, then into bread crumb mixture, coating well. Arrange in a greased 13"x9" baking pan. Pour any remaining butter mixture over chops; sprinkle with remaining crumbs. Add salt and pepper to taste; drizzle with olive oil. Bake at 375 degrees for 45 to 50 minutes, until golden and tender. When serving, scrape up golden bits on bottom of baking pan and spoon over chops. Serves 4 to 6.

Try something new instead of carving a pumpkin.
A paper doily will leave a delicate lacy pattern
when you use it as a template for painting on your pumpkin.

Chicken Tetrazzini

Debbie Musick
Yukon, OK

This recipe was originally made by "Aunt" Cathryn, my mother's closest and dearest friend. Now it's become a dish that's always a part of our family gatherings.

1 onion, chopped
1 T. butter
2 10-3/4 oz. cans cream of
  mushroom soup
2 10-3/4 oz. cans cream of
  chicken soup
8-oz. jar sharp pasteurized
  process cheese spread
1/2 c. milk
1/2 c. water
1 t. curry powder
1/4 t. dried thyme
1/4 t. dried oregano
1/8 t. dried basil
2 7-oz. pkgs. elbow macaroni,
  prepared
5 c. chicken, cooked and cubed
2-oz. jar pimentos, drained
8-oz. pkg. shredded Cheddar
  cheese

Sauté onion in butter; add soups, cheese spread, milk, water, curry powder and seasonings. Stir in macaroni; mix in chicken. Spoon into 2 lightly greased 13"x9" baking pans; sprinkle with pimentos and shredded cheese. Bake at 350 degrees for 45 minutes. Serves 12 to 16.

Wrap a plain glass hurricane lantern with vintage-style Halloween postcards copied onto sheets of vellum. Slip a tealight inside for a magical glow.

Italian 3-Cheese Stuffed Shells

Melanie McNew
Cameron, MO

A super dish for any get-together and it's so simple to whip up.

1 lb. ground beef
1 c. onion, chopped
1 clove garlic, minced
2 c. hot water
12-oz. can tomato paste
1 T. instant beef bouillon
1-1/2 t. dried oregano

16-oz. container cottage cheese
8-oz. pkg. shredded mozzarella
  cheese, divided
1/2 c. grated Parmesan cheese
1 egg, beaten
24 jumbo pasta shells, cooked

Brown beef, onion and garlic in a large skillet over medium-high heat; drain. Stir in water, tomato paste, bouillon and oregano; simmer over medium heat for about 30 minutes. Stir together cottage cheese, one cup mozzarella, Parmesan cheese and egg in a medium bowl; mix well. Stuff cooked shells with cheese mixture; arrange in a greased 13"x9" baking pan. Pour beef mixture over shells. Cover and bake at 350 degrees for 30 minutes. Uncover; sprinkle with remaining mozzarella cheese. Bake for an additional 5 minutes, until cheese melts. Makes 6 to 8 servings.

Haunted window decorations...simply cut out shapes from black car-window film! Apply cut-outs to the window, rubbing to smooth out any air bubbles. To remove, gently peel off.

Creamy Shrimp Fettuccine

Debbie Desormeaux
Lafayette, LA

A fabulous casserole for seafood lovers! I usually divide the ingredients between 2 casserole dishes, then freeze before baking. When ready to enjoy, thaw completely and proceed with directions.

1 onion, chopped
1 green pepper, chopped
1/2 c. butter
1-1/2 T. all-purpose flour
1/2 t. Cajun seasoning
1 t. green onion, minced
8-oz. pkg. pasteurized process
  cheese spread, cubed
1 c. half-and-half
1 clove garlic, minced
1 lb. shrimp, peeled, cleaned
  and chopped
12-oz. pkg. fettuccine, cooked
Garnish: grated Parmesan
  cheese

Sauté onion and pepper in butter over medium heat. Reduce heat and add flour; cook 15 minutes, stirring often. Add Cajun seasoning and green onion; cook for several minutes longer. Add cheese spread, half-and-half and garlic; cook until cheese melts. Stir in shrimp; cook an additional 10 minutes. Combine sauce with cooked pasta and pour into a greased 2-quart casserole dish. Sprinkle with Parmesan cheese; bake at 350 degrees for 15 to 30 minutes, until bubbly. Serves 8.

Slip artificial fall leaves under silverware on your autumn dinner table...so pretty.

Italian Chicken & Artichokes

Nicole Kasprzyk
Turlock, CA

This is one of the first recipes I learned to make and it's still my all-time favorite.

8-oz. container sour cream
10-3/4 oz. can cream of
  chicken soup
1/2 c. white wine or
  chicken broth
1/2 c. shredded
  mozzarella cheese
1/2 c. shredded
  Parmesan cheese
2 T. butter

2 cloves garlic, minced
4 boneless, skinless chicken
  breasts, sliced into
  2-inch strips
14-oz. jar marinated
  artichokes, drained
16-oz. pkg. rainbow
  rotini, cooked
Garnish: shredded
  Parmesan cheese

Combine sour cream, soup, wine or broth and cheeses in a bowl; set aside. Melt butter in a large, heavy skillet over medium heat; sauté garlic for 30 seconds. Add chicken and cook for 5 to 7 minutes, until golden. Pour sour cream mixture over chicken; cover and cook over low heat for 10 minutes. Add artichokes; heat for an additional 5 minutes. Serve sauce and chicken over cooked pasta; sprinkle with Parmesan cheese. Serves 4 to 6.

Summer's loss seems little, dear,
on days like these.

-Ernest Dowson

Southwestern Casserole

Bobbi Carney
Arvada, CO

The kids will love this...grown-ups too!

2 lbs. ground beef
1 onion, chopped
2 8-oz. cans enchilada sauce
2 15-oz. cans chili beans
   with sauce

13-1/2 oz. pkg. tortilla chips,
   divided
8-oz. pkg. shredded Cheddar
   cheese
Garnish: sour cream

Brown beef and onion together in a skillet over medium heat; drain. Stir in enchilada sauce and beans. Coarsely break up tortilla chips, reserving 1/2 cup. Arrange remaining chips in a lightly greased 13"x9" baking pan; spread meat mixture on top. Sprinkle with reserved tortilla chips and Cheddar cheese. Bake, covered, at 350 degrees for 30 minutes. Remove from oven; garnish with sour cream. Serve immediately. Serves 6.

Turn a porch into a gathering place. Add a comfy chair or two, table and cozy blanket for when the temperature drops. It's an outdoor room just right for watching the leaves turn colors.

Chill Chaser Chili Bake

Tisha Brown
Elizabethtown, PA

A quick, hot meal for busy weeknights. It's filled with scrumptious layers of cheese and chili!

2 c. biscuit baking mix
2/3 c. water
3 c. chili with beans, divided

1/2 lb. hot dogs, sliced
8-oz. pkg. shredded Cheddar
 cheese

Blend together baking mix and water in a medium bowl until smooth. Shape into a ball and roll out dough to a 1/4-inch thick circle; set aside. Spread half the chili in the bottom of a lightly greased 1-1/2 quart casserole dish. Arrange sliced hot dogs over chili; top with cheese, then with remaining chili. Lay dough over top; cut several slits in dough to vent steam. Bake at 350 degrees for 15 to 25 minutes, or until crust is golden. Makes 4 servings.

A brisk autumn afternoon is the best time to spend an entire day outside. Go on a nature walk, apple picking, hiking, craft-making...make sure there's something for everyone to enjoy.

Buttermilk Chicken

Susan Lewis
Lynn Haven, FL

A classic, old-fashioned dish...great for company.

1-1/2 c. buttermilk, divided
3/4 c. all-purpose flour
1-1/2 t. salt
1/2 t. pepper
2-1/2 lbs. boneless, skinless
   chicken breast, cubed

1/4 c. margarine, melted
10-3/4 oz. can cream of
   chicken soup

Pour 1/4 cup buttermilk in a bowl; set aside. Combine flour, salt and pepper in another bowl. Dip chicken into buttermilk, then coat with flour mixture. Set aside. Pour margarine into an ungreased 13"x9" baking pan; arrange chicken in pan. Bake at 375 degrees for 30 minutes. Turn chicken over; bake an additional 15 minutes. Blend remaining buttermilk with soup; pour over chicken. Bake for 15 minutes, or until chicken is tender. Serves 4.

Juicy Buttermilk Chicken is ideal for taking along on an autumn hike and picnic. Wrapped in wax paper, it tucks nicely into a pail along with some fresh fruit and homemade rolls.

Garlic Pot Roast

Nancy Girard
Chesapeake, VA

*I make this dish on the first chilly fall day. It smells heavenly
as it's cooking and never fails to please my family.*

7 cloves garlic, divided
3 to 4-lb. beef chuck roast
1 T. oil
1 onion, chopped

1 c. beef broth
1 c. red wine or beef broth
salt and pepper to taste

Cut 4 garlic cloves into thin slivers; set aside. Cut small slits in roast;
insert a garlic sliver in each slit. Brown roast on all sides in oil in a
stockpot; remove roast and set aside. Chop remaining garlic. Add
onion and chopped garlic to stockpot; sauté until golden, about
10 minutes. Return roast to stockpot; add broth, wine or broth, salt
and pepper to taste. Bring to a boil; reduce heat. Cover and simmer
until tender, about 2-1/2 hours, turning occasionally. Remove roast to
a serving platter; cover loosely with aluminum foil. To make sauce,
skim and discard fat from cooking liquid. Bring remaining liquid to a
boil and cook until reduced to about 1-1/2 cups. Serve sauce with
sliced pot roast. Makes 8 servings.

An oh-so-easy side to serve with dinner...layer olives,
feta cheese cubes and marinated artichoke hearts
in a stemware glass.

Stuffed Cabbage Rolls

Alexis Mauriello
Richardson, TX

The aroma of homestyle cooking fills the house as this is simmering.
It's hard to wait until it's done!

12 leaves cabbage
1-1/4 lbs. ground beef
1 c. prepared rice
1 onion, chopped
1 egg, beaten
1/2 t. poultry seasoning or
    dried thyme

2 T. oil
2 8-oz. cans tomato sauce
1 T. brown sugar, packed
1/4 c. water
1 T. lemon juice or vinegar

Cover cabbage leaves with boiling water; let stand for 5 minutes or, until leaves are limp. Drain and set aside. Combine ground beef, rice, onion, egg and poultry seasoning or thyme; mix well. Place equal portions of meat mixture in center of each cabbage leaf. Fold sides of each leaf over meat mixture; roll up and fasten with a toothpick. Heat oil in a large skillet over medium heat; add rolls and sauté until golden. Pour tomato sauce into skillet. Combine brown sugar, water and lemon juice or vinegar; stir into tomato sauce. Cover and simmer for one hour, basting occasionally. Makes 6 servings.

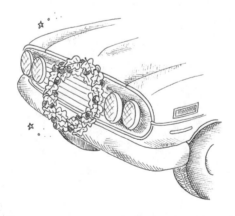

Tie a fall wreath bursting with color on the
front grill of your car...just because!

Penne & Sausage

Holly Paskell
Galveston, TX

*For a twist, I sometimes add cheese tortellini in the boiling water
while the penne is cooking. Two pasta types add a nice touch.*

19.76-oz. pkg. mild or hot
   Italian sausage links
16-oz. pkg. penne pasta,
   uncooked
15-oz. can Italian stewed
   tomatoes with juice, chopped

1 pt. half-and-half
1 c. grated Parmesan cheese
1 T. fresh rosemary, chopped
salt and pepper to taste

Remove sausage from casings; brown in a skillet. Drain and set aside.
Cook pasta according to package directions; drain and return to pan.
Toss together sausage, cooked pasta and remaining ingredients; cook
until heated through. Makes 6 servings.

Fun-filled snacks for kids big or little.
Fill waffle cones with sliced fresh fruit, then drizzle fruit
with puréed strawberries. Yum!

Steak & Spinach Pinwheels

Vickie

Such a pretty presentation for special occasions.

1 to 1-1/4 lb. beef flank steak or top round steak, halved lengthwise
3/4 t. lemon-pepper seasoning
1/4 t. salt

8 slices bacon, partially cooked
10-oz. pkg. frozen chopped spinach, thawed and drained
2 T. dry bread crumbs
1/2 t. dried thyme

With a sharp knife, score both pieces of steak in a diamond pattern with cuts one-inch apart. Repeat on other side. Place one piece of steak between 2 lengths of plastic wrap; pound lightly into a 10"x6" rectangle. Repeat with second piece. Blend seasoning and salt; sprinkle each steak evenly with half of seasoning mixture. Arrange 4 slices of bacon lengthwise on each; set aside. Combine remaining ingredients in a bowl; spread half of spinach mixture over each steak. Starting at a short end, roll up each steak. Place toothpicks at one-inch intervals on rolled-up steak to form 6, one-inch pinwheels. Slice between toothpicks. Slide 2 pinwheels carefully onto each skewer. Cook on grill over medium-high heat to desired doneness, about 6 to 7 minutes for medium doneness. Serves 6.

Use mini Indian corn cobs as a flower frog.
Place the ears in a clear glass vase, fill the vase with water and add flowers. How clever!

Tarragon Chicken

Elizabeth VanEtten
Warwick, NY

*I serve this with hot buttered noodles or rice
alongside steamed broccoli or carrots.*

4 to 6 boneless, skinless
   chicken breasts
salt and pepper to taste
1/4 to 1/2 c. all-purpose flour,
   divided
1/4 c. butter

1 to 2 T. onion, chopped
1/4 c. white wine or
   chicken broth
1 T. fresh tarragon, chopped
1/2 c. chicken broth
1/4 c. whipping cream

Rub chicken with salt and pepper; dredge in 1/4 cup flour, reserving remaining flour. Set aside. Melt butter in a skillet over medium heat; add chicken. Cook chicken on both sides until golden; remove from skillet. Stir in onion; sauté until translucent. Pour in wine or chicken broth; cook until bubbly. Add remaining flour; sprinkle with tarragon. Stir in chicken broth until smooth; return chicken to mixture. Cook until heated through; stir in cream. Serves 4 to 6.

When it comes to fun & games, keep it simple. Enjoy old-fashioned favorites like ring toss, pin the tail on the donkey, hide & seek and duck-duck-goose.

Super-Simple Lasagna

Donna Hoerner
Good Hope, IL

Just the thing to take to a tailgating get-together.

28-oz. jar spaghetti sauce
1-1/2 lbs. ground beef, browned
   and drained
4-oz. can mushroom stems and
   pieces, drained

16-oz. pkg. lasagna, cooked
8-oz. pkg. shredded mozzarella
   cheese
1 c. shredded Cheddar cheese
1/4 c. grated Parmesan cheese

Mix together sauce, ground beef and mushrooms. Spread a thin
layer of sauce mixture in a lightly greased 13"x9" baking dish. Layer
with lasagna, mozzarella and Cheddar. Continue layering until all
ingredients are used, ending with shredded cheeses and Parmesan.
Bake at 350 degrees for approximately 45 minutes. Serves 6 to 8.

A grandmother pretends she doesn't know
who you are on Halloween.

-Erma Bombeck

Mom's Sicilian Pot Roast

Barbara Rannazzisi
Gainesville, VA

We start this dish early in the morning so it's cooking while appetizers are nibbled on during football games. Served with a crisp salad and garlic bread, life doesn't get any better than this!

4-lb. rolled rump beef roast
2 T. garlic-flavored olive oil
2 22-oz. cans plum tomatoes
12-oz. can Italian tomato sauce
1 c. water
1 T. garlic, minced
1/2 c. dried oregano

1/3 c. dried basil
1/2 c. dried parsley
1-1/2 t. salt
1/2 t. pepper
Optional: 1/4 c. all-purpose
    flour, 2 c. hot water
prepared rotini pasta

Brown roast slowly in oil in a Dutch oven. Add tomatoes, tomato sauce, water, garlic and seasonings to Dutch oven. Heat to boiling; cover. Reduce heat and simmer 2-1/2 hours or until tender, turning occasionally. Remove roast from Dutch oven; cut into serving-size slices. Return meat to Dutch oven; simmer, uncovered, another 30 minutes. If sauce is not thick enough, combine flour and water, stirring until dissolved. Gradually add flour mixture into sauce, a little at a time, until sauce thickens. To serve, place prepared pasta on a large platter; top with sauce and sliced meat. Serves 8 to 10.

String dried Chinese lantern flowers to dress up a mantel for fall. Their bright orange color really brings the autumn colors inside!

Baked Steak with Gravy

Amy Halstead
Winfield, WV

As a wedding present, a dear friend hand-copied 75 of her "tried & true" recipes...this is one. Every time I make one of her special dishes, I smile and think loving thoughts of Miss Nancy.

1 c. all-purpose flour
1/8 t. salt
1/8 t. pepper
6 to 8 beef cube steaks
1 t. butter

2 10-3/4 oz. cans cream of
   mushroom soup
2-1/2 c. water
Optional: 4-oz. can sliced
   mushrooms, drained

Mix flour, salt and pepper in a shallow bowl. Dredge meat in flour mixture. Melt butter in a skillet over medium heat; add meat and brown on both sides. Arrange meat in a lightly greased 13"x9" baking pan; set aside. Combine soup, water and mushrooms, if using, in a bowl. Pour soup mixture over meat; cover with aluminum foil. Bake at 325 degrees for 45 to 50 minutes. Uncover; bake an additional 15 minutes. Serves 6 to 8.

Serve warm or chilled cider in old-fashioned Mason jars! Setting the jars inside wire drink carriers makes it easy to tote them from kitchen to harvest table.

Chicken Noodle Casserole

Cathy Wolf
Canton, TX

A great recipe for family reunions or church suppers.
I usually double it!

3 to 4-lb. chicken
3 to 4 boneless, skinless
   chicken breasts
2 cubes chicken bouillon
2 onions, diced and divided
salt to taste
1-1/2 t. lemon-pepper seasoning
1-1/2 t. garlic powder
2 stalks celery, diced
8-oz. pkg. sliced mushrooms
3 to 4 slices bacon, chopped
6-oz. can tomato paste
10-3/4 oz. can cream of
   mushroom soup
10-3/4 oz. can cream of
   chicken soup

10-3/4 oz. can tomato soup
2 14-1/2-oz. cans
   chicken broth
15-1/2 oz. can stewed
   tomatoes, drained
16-oz. pkg. wide egg
   noodles, uncooked
16-oz. pkg. shredded
   Cheddar cheese
16-oz. pkg. shredded
   Monterey Jack cheese
11-oz. can sliced black olives,
   drained
Garnish: grated Parmesan
   cheese

Cover all chicken with water in a large pot. Add bouillon, one onion and seasonings. Simmer until very tender, adding water as necessary to cover chicken. Remove chicken; reserve broth. Discard bones and skin; cut chicken into bite-size pieces. Set aside. Combine celery and remaining onion with 1/2 cup reserved broth; microwave on high setting for 4 minutes. Place celery mixture in a large saucepan; add mushrooms and bacon. Sauté for 5 minutes; remove bacon and reserve for another use. Add tomato paste, soups, canned broth and tomatoes; simmer over low heat for 15 to 20 minutes, until vegetables are tender. Set aside. Bring remaining reserved broth to a boil; add noodles and cook according to package directions. Drain, reserving one cup broth; set aside. Mix cheeses together; set aside. Combine noodles, vegetable mixture, chicken and olives in a large bowl; mix well, adding reserved broth if mixture seems dry. In a greased 13"x9" baking pan layer noodle mixture alternately with cheese mixture, ending with cheese. Bake at 350 degrees for 30 minutes, until bubbly and cheese is golden. Garnish with Parmesan. Serves 8 to 10.

Homestyle Meatloaf

Shirley Condy
Plainview, NY

No one will guess pretzels are the secret ingredient to this old-fashioned favorite.

2 lbs. ground beef
1 egg, beaten
3/4 c. catsup
1/4 c. milk

1 onion, chopped
1 c. pretzels, crushed
Garnish: catsup

Combine all ingredients except garnish; mix well. Place in a greased 9"x5" loaf pan. Bake at 350 degrees for one hour; top with additional catsup during last 15 minutes. Makes 6 to 8 servings.

Combine your favorite food with family & friends...at a drive-in movie in your own backyard! Drape a giant painter's cloth outside for the movie screen, then rent projection equipment for your favorite DVDs and videos. Sure to be a hit!

Bacon-Mushroom Spaghetti Pie

Kathy Price
Quincy, MI

The bacon gives this dish its special flavor.

1/2 lb. ground beef
1/2 c. onion, chopped
7-oz. can mushroom stems and
   pieces, drained
14-1/2 oz. can diced tomatoes
10-3/4 oz. can tomato soup
1/2 t. pepper

1/2 t. dried, minced garlic
8-oz. pkg. shredded Cheddar
   cheese, divided
8-oz. pkg. spaghetti, cooked
4 slices bacon, crisply cooked
   and crumbled

Combine ground beef, onion and mushrooms in a large skillet. Cook over medium heat until beef is browned, stirring occasionally. Drain. Reduce heat; stir in tomatoes, tomato soup, pepper and garlic. Add 1-1/2 cups shredded cheese, stirring until melted. Add cooked spaghetti and bacon to beef mixture; toss to combine. Pour into a greased 2-quart casserole dish. Cover and bake at 350 degrees for 30 minutes, or until bubbly and heated through. Uncover; sprinkle with remaining cheese. Let stand for 5 to 10 minutes, until cheese is melted. Serves 4 to 6.

·Wrap silverware in lengths of raffia, ribbon or homespun...pretty enough for any harvest table...inside or out.

Super-Easy Stuffed Peppers

Tabetha Moore
New Braunfels, TX

My husband says these are the best stuffed peppers! Depending on the size of the peppers, there may be ground beef mixture remaining. When there is, I just sprinkle it with a little cheese and serve alongside tortilla chips for a quick lunch.

4 green peppers, tops removed
1 lb. ground beef
1 onion, diced
3 T. Italian seasoning
1 clove garlic, pressed
3 c. prepared rice

26-oz. can spaghetti sauce, divided
salt and pepper to taste
Garnish: grated Parmesan cheese

Bring a large saucepan of water to a boil; add peppers and boil until tender. Drain and set aside. Brown ground beef with onion in a skillet; drain. Add Italian seasoning and garlic. Combine ground beef mixture, prepared rice and all except 1/2 cup spaghetti sauce in a large bowl. Add salt and pepper to taste. Arrange peppers in a lightly greased 8"x8" baking pan. Fill peppers completely with ground beef mixture, spooning any extra mixture between peppers. Top with reserved sauce. Lightly cover with aluminum foil; bake at 400 degrees for 30 to 45 minutes. Sprinkle with Parmesan cheese. Serves 4.

Use bread bowls to serve up sides, salads or soups this harvest season. Simply hollow out a few small round loaves of bread and fill.

Autumn Treats

Harvest Celebration Cake

Kerri Urbanczyk
Munday, TX

Such a pretty cake and so delicious.

1-1/2 c. sugar
1/2 c. brown sugar, packed
2 t. baking soda
1/2 t. salt
2 t. cinnamon
1/4 t. nutmeg
1/4 t. ground ginger
1 c. oil

1/2 t. vanilla extract
4 eggs
2 c. all-purpose flour
15-oz. can pumpkin
1 apple, cored, peeled
　and chopped
1/2 c. chopped nuts

Combine sugar, brown sugar, baking soda, salt and spices; mix well.
Stir in oil, vanilla and eggs. Add flour, 1/2 cup at a time, beating after
each addition. Mix in pumpkin; stir in apple and nuts. Pour into a
greased and floured Bundt® pan; bake at 350 degrees for one hour. Let
cool; spread with icing. Serves 10 to 12.

Frosty Vanilla Icing:

16-oz. pkg. powdered sugar
1/2 c. butter, softened
2 t. vanilla extract

8-oz. pkg. cream cheese,
　softened

Combine all ingredients until smooth and a good spreading
consistency.

Fill the night with eerie
music...pick up a CD at a
local party store to really set
the Halloween mood!

Ginger-Pumpkin Mousse

Deanna Lyons
Gooseberry Patch

Top with a dollop of whipped cream and a sprinkle of cinnamon
or nutmeg for an elegant finishing touch.

4 pasteurized eggs
7 T. sugar
1 T. unflavored gelatin
1-1/2 c. canned pumpkin

3/4 t. cinnamon
1/2 t. ground ginger
1/4 t. nutmeg
1 c. whipping cream

Beat eggs and sugar together in a medium bowl until thick; blend in
gelatin. Stir in pumpkin and spices; set aside. Using an electric mixer
on high speed, whip cream into soft peaks in a small bowl. Fold cream
into pumpkin mixture. Chill for 4 hours. Serves 4 to 6.

Create a spooky greeting for trick-or-treaters...it's simple!
Paint a dried bottle gourd white, use a black felt tip pen to
add a face. Arrange several in a straw-filled wagon.

Pumpkin Bread Pudding

Pamela Stump
Chino Hills, CA

This recipe is easy to make and so warming on a frosty fall day.

4-1/2 c. croissants, cut
   into large cubes
6 eggs
4 egg yolks
1 c. brown sugar, packed
   and divided
2 t. cinnamon
2 t. ground cloves
2 t. nutmeg

2 t. ground ginger
1/8 t. salt
2 t. vanilla extract
2 c. milk
1 pt. whipping cream
15-oz. can pumpkin
1/2 c. pecan halves
Optional: whipped cream

Arrange croissant cubes evenly in a 13"x9" baking pan sprayed with
non-stick vegetable spray. Place eggs and yolks in a bowl; beat with
an electric mixer on low speed until well blended. Add 1/2 cup brown
sugar, spices, salt and vanilla; mix until combined. Add milk, cream
and pumpkin; mix well. Pour over croissant cubes; stir briefly so that
cubes are moistened. Sprinkle remaining brown sugar and pecans on
top of cubes. Bake at 350 degrees until custard is set and top is
golden, about 45 minutes. Serve warm or at room temperature; top
with a dollop of whipped cream, if desired. Serves 10.

Set plump sugar pumpkins in a vintage-style plant stand.
Great for a buffet table during autumn!

Sweet Potato Pound Cake

Cindy Spears
Keithville, LA

This old-fashioned dessert will scent your kitchen with the aroma of cinnamon and spice as it bakes.

3 c. all-purpose flour
2 t. baking powder
1 t. baking soda
1 t. salt
1-1/2 t. cinnamon
1/4 t. nutmeg
1/4 t. mace

1 c. butter, softened
1-1/2 c. sugar
1/4 c. brown sugar, packed
2-1/2 c. sweet potatoes, peeled,
    cooked and mashed
4 eggs
1 T. vanilla extract

Whisk together flour, baking powder, baking soda, salt and spices in a medium bowl. Set aside. Combine butter and sugars together in a large bowl; using an electric mixer, beat on high speed until fluffy. Beat in sweet potatoes; add eggs, one at a time. Add flour mixture one-third at a time on low speed; beat in vanilla. Spoon into a Bundt® pan sprayed with non-stick vegetable spray. Bake at 350 degrees for one hour, or until cake tests done. Serves 10 to 12.

Use a drill with a 1/2-inch bit to drill holes in any design in a hollowed-out pumpkin. Fill each pumpkin with a strand of battery-operated tiny white lights for a lovely glow.

Turtle Cookies

Cheri Emery
Quincy, IL

Ideal for placing in a lined vintage picnic tin...any hostess will love them!

18-1/2 oz. pkg. chocolate
   fudge cake mix
1 T. water

2 T. oil
2 eggs
1/2-lb. pkg. pecan halves

Combine dry cake mix, water, oil and eggs; mix well and set aside. Arrange pecans in clusters of 3 on greased baking sheets; reserve any leftover pecans for another recipe. Shape dough into one-inch balls; center each on a cluster of pecans and flatten slightly. Bake for 8 to 10 minutes at 375 degrees. Let cool; spread with Chocolate Frosting. Makes about 2 dozen.

Chocolate Frosting:

1 T. oil
2 T. baking cocoa
1/2 t. vanilla extract

1 c. powdered sugar
2 T. milk

Mix oil and cocoa. Add vanilla, sugar and milk alternately to make a consistency good for spreading.

Tie a stack of 3 big cookies together with a length of jute and set in the middle of a dinner plate or inside a lunchbox for a sweet surprise!

Caramel Flan

Elizabeth Blackstone
Racine, WI

You won't be disappointed!

3/4 c. sugar
12-oz. can evaporated milk
14-oz. can sweetened
   condensed milk

3 eggs
1 T. vanilla extract
Garnish: whipped cream,
   sliced fruit

Sprinkle sugar in a small, heavy saucepan. Heat and stir constantly over medium-low heat for 3 to 4 minutes, until melted and golden. Quickly pour into an ungreased 9" pie plate; swirl to coat bottom and sides. Use caution...the caramelized sugar is extremely hot. Combine milks, eggs and vanilla in a blender; cover and blend for one minute. Pour over sugar in pie plate. Set pie plate in a large roasting pan; fill roasting pan with one inch of warm water. Bake at 325 degrees for 45 to 50 minutes, or until a knife inserted near center comes out clean. Cool on a wire rack for one hour; refrigerate for 4 to 6 hours, or until firm. To serve, quickly dip the pie plate into hot water; run a knife around the edge and invert onto a rimmed serving plate. Cut into wedges and garnish as desired with whipped cream and fruit. Makes 8 servings.

Buy several yards of 2-inch wide twill ribbon to stamp fall greetings on! Use alphabet rubber stamps and a fabric stamp pad, then stamp away. Tie the ribbon on greeting cards or drape like garland.

Pumpkin Pie Cake

Kim Berndt
Andover, MN

The best-tasting dessert...forget about having any left over!

18-1/2 oz. pkg. yellow
   cake mix, divided
1/2 c. butter, softened
4 eggs, divided
29-oz. can pumpkin

1/2 c. brown sugar, packed
1/2 c. sugar
2/3 c. evaporated milk
1-1/2 t. cinnamon

Set aside one cup cake mix for topping. Combine remaining cake mix, butter and one egg in a medium bowl. Mix well and pour into a greased 13"x9" baking pan. In another bowl, mix together pumpkin, remaining eggs, sugars, milk and cinnamon; pour over cake batter. Sprinkle topping over pumpkin layer. Bake at 350 degrees for 50 to 60 minutes. Serves 6 to 8.

Topping:

1 c. reserved yellow cake mix
1/2 c. sugar

1/2 c. chopped walnuts
1/4 c. butter, softened

Mix all ingredients together until crumbly.

An old-fashioned dough bowl filled with pumpkin-shaped candles or yellow and orange votives creates a quick & easy table centerpiece in no time!

Cinnamon Flop Cake

Vicky Paul
Imperial, MO

I found this recipe years ago in a magazine featuring Pennsylvania Dutch recipes. It's so easy and so good…rises in the middle when baking, then flops when taken out of the oven.

1-1/2 c. sugar
2 T. butter, melted
1 egg
1 c. milk
2 c. all-purpose flour

2 t. baking powder
1/4 t. salt
1 c. brown sugar, packed
1/4 c. butter, chilled and diced
1-1/2 t. cinnamon

Place sugar, melted butter, egg and milk in a large mixing bowl; beat with an electric mixer on medium speed for 2 minutes. Stir in flour, baking powder and salt. Spread in a greased 8"x8" baking pan. Sprinkle with brown sugar; dot with diced butter and sprinkle with cinnamon. Bake at 425 degrees for about 35 minutes, until a toothpick inserted in center comes out clean. Cool 10 minutes; cut into squares. Serve warm. Makes 6 servings.

Turn "plain" caramel apples into works of art! Drizzle with melted white and semi-sweet chocolate, then roll in crushed nuts while the chocolate is still warm. So yummy!

Autumn Treats

Pumpkin Sandwich Cookies

Mary Patenaude
Griswold, CT

These are cookies you'll want to make all season long.

2 eggs, beaten
15-oz. can pumpkin
2 c. sugar
1 c. oil
2 t. vanilla extract

4 c. all-purpose flour
1 T. plus 1 t. baking powder
2 t. cinnamon
1/2 t. baking soda
1/4 t. salt

Combine eggs, pumpkin, sugar, oil and vanilla in a large bowl; set aside. In another bowl, stir together flour, baking powder, cinnamon, baking soda and salt. Add to pumpkin mixture; stir well. Drop by rounded teaspoonfuls onto ungreased baking sheets. Flatten each to a 2-inch circle. Bake at 350 degrees for 8 to 10 minutes, or until set and bottoms are golden. Cool on wire racks. Spread half the cookies with filling and top with remaining cookies flat-side down. Store in refrigerator. Makes 3 dozen.

Filling:

8-oz. pkg. cream cheese,
   softened
1/2 c. butter, softened

16-oz. pkg. powdered sugar
1 t. vanilla extract

Beat cream cheese and butter in a medium bowl. Add powdered sugar and vanilla; beat until smooth.

Fill a thermos with warm spiced cider, and a basket or tin with cookies. Head out for a lazy drive down a country road...what a way to spend a fall day.

Dutch Nutmeg Cookies

Mary Walsh
Valencia, CA

Oh-so-easy slice & bake cookies.

1 c. butter, softened
1/4 t. baking soda
1 t. cinnamon
1/2 t. nutmeg
1/8 t. ground cloves

1 c. sugar
1/2 c. chopped nuts
2 c. all-purpose flour
1/4 c. sour cream

Combine butter, baking soda and spices; blend until fluffy. Gradually add sugar; beat until fluffy. Stir in nuts. Add flour alternately with sour cream; mix well. Shape into a 6"x2" roll. Wrap in wax paper, then aluminum foil; freeze overnight. Thaw slightly; cut into 1/8-inch thick slices. Place on lightly greased baking sheets. Bake at 375 degrees for 15 to 20 minutes, until golden. Let cool on wire racks. Makes 4 dozen.

Conjure up some spooky Halloween touches...stack cookies or arrange cupcakes on a black hobnail cake stand.

Pulled Molasses Taffy

Tanya Payzant
Nova Scotia, Canada

An old-fashioned favorite that's just as much fun to make today!

1-1/4 c. brown sugar, packed
1/3 c. molasses
1/4 c. water
2 T. cider vinegar

2 t. butter
1/4 t. baking soda
1 t. warm water

Place brown sugar, molasses, water, vinegar and butter in a deep, heavy saucepan; bring to a boil over medium heat. Cook without stirring for about 8 minutes, until mixture reaches the soft-crack stage, or 270 to 289 degrees on a candy thermometer. Dissolve baking soda in water; stir into mixture and cook for an additional 5 minutes. With a metal spatula, fold edges toward the center. Using buttered hands, pull taffy between 2 people, until it begins to harden. Cut into small pieces using buttered scissors. Store in an airtight container for up to 2 weeks. Makes 2 cups before taffy is pulled.

Put together a cookie basket for a dear friend.
Fill it with tubs of frosting, jimmies, sparkly sugars, little candies and lots of unfrosted cookies. The perfect ingredients for an afternoon of fun in the kitchen!

Creamy Pumpkin Fudge

Amy Woods
Collinsville, TX

A treat any teacher will love to receive. Wrap individual squares in wax paper and tuck inside an apple basket.

1-1/2 c. sugar
2/3 c. evaporated milk
1/2 c. canned pumpkin
2 T. butter
1-1/2 t. pumpkin pie spice
1/2 t. salt

2 c. mini marshmallows
12-oz. pkg. white
   chocolate chips
1/2 c. chopped walnuts, toasted
1 t. vanilla extract

Butter sides of a heavy medium saucepan. Combine sugar, evaporated milk, pumpkin, butter, pumpkin pie spice and salt in saucepan. Bring to a boil over medium heat; boil for 12 minutes, stirring constantly. Remove from heat. Add marshmallows, chocolate chips, walnuts and vanilla; stir until melted. Pour into an aluminum foil-lined, greased 8"x8" baking pan; chill until firm. Cut into one-inch squares. Store in an airtight container in refrigerator. Makes about 4 dozen pieces.

A tin of sweet & salty treats is nice for nibbling on during the Thanksgiving Day football frenzy. Use a metallic pen to write the name of the treat on a red or golden leaf and secure the leaf to the tin with a length of jute or raffia.

Mini Maple-Pear Cobblers

Karen Pilcher
Burleson, TX

*Serve warm with whipped cream, drizzled with
additional maple syrup...so good.*

3 lbs. pears, cored, peeled
   and quartered
2/3 c. maple syrup
2 T. all-purpose flour
1 t. vanilla extract

1/4 t. nutmeg
2 T. butter, sliced
Garnish: melted butter,
   sugar, nutmeg

Combine pears, syrup, flour, vanilla and nutmeg in a bowl; mix
well. Divide among 6 lightly greased custard cups; place a pat of
butter on top of each. Bake at 425 degrees for 18 to 20 minutes.
Drop topping by spoonfuls onto hot pear mixture. Brush with melted
butter; sprinkle with sugar and nutmeg. Bake at 425 degrees for an
additional 14 minutes, or until golden and firm to the touch.
Serves 6.

Topping:

1-1/2 c. all-purpose flour
2-1/4 t. baking powder
1/4 t. nutmeg
6 T. butter

9 T. whipping cream
9 T. maple syrup
1 t. vanilla extract

Combine flour, baking powder and nutmeg in a food processor. Add
butter and pulse until fine crumbs form. Add cream, syrup and vanilla;
process until combined.

Cinnamon Jumbles

Emily Dachel
Hudson, WI

This yummy recipe is found inside a cookbook my mom created for my sister and me when we each married.

1/2 c. shortening
1/2 c. butter, softened
1-1/4 c. sugar, divided
1 egg
3/4 c. buttermilk

1 t. vanilla extract
2 c. all-purpose flour
1/2 t. baking soda
1/2 t. salt
1 t. cinnamon

Mix shortening, butter, one cup sugar and egg thoroughly. Stir in buttermilk and vanilla; set aside. Blend together flour, baking soda and salt; mix with shortening mixture. Chill for about 2 hours. Drop by rounded teaspoonfuls, about 2-inches apart, on lightly greased baking sheets. Mix cinnamon and remaining sugar; sprinkle onto cookies. Bake for 8 to 10 minutes at 400 degrees. Makes 4 dozen.

Cookies are easy to wrap and tote for any autumn gathering...from a tailgating get-together to a picnic in the country.

Honey-Pumpkin Pie

Sharon Demers
Dolores, CO

Whenever I can, I make this pie with farm-fresh eggs
and honey from a local beekeeper.

15-oz. can pumpkin
3/4 c. honey
1/2 t. salt
1 t. cinnamon
1/2 t. ground ginger
1/4 t. ground cloves

1/4 t. nutmeg
3 eggs
2/3 c. evaporated milk
1/2 c. milk
9-inch pie crust

Stir together pumpkin, honey, salt and spices in a large mixing bowl. Add eggs and mix well; stir in milks. Place pie crust in a 9" pie plate; flute edges forming a high rim to hold pumpkin filling. Do not pierce crust. Place pie crust on oven rack; pour in filling. Bake at 375 degrees for 55 to 60 minutes, or until set. Let cool before serving. Makes 6 to 8 servings.

Dress up Honey-Pumpkin Pie with a smile! Roll out remaining pie crust dough and cut out 3 triangles...2 for eyes, one for a nose. Place them on an unbaked pie. Add a smile with a crescent moon-shaped portion of dough; bake as directed.

Apple Crunch Pie

Colleen Farley
Huntingdon Valley, PA

*Every October I have a Halloween fall festival in my backyard. All of
my girlfriends come running for a slice of this apple pie!*

2/3 c. sugar
1/4 c. all-purpose flour
1/2 t. nutmeg
1/2 t. cinnamon
1/8 t. salt

5 Granny Smith apples, cored,
   peeled and sliced
9-inch pie crust
Optional: 1/2 c. cranberries
Garnish: cinnamon-sugar

Whisk sugar, flour, nutmeg, cinnamon and salt in a large bowl. Stir in
apples and cranberries, if using; spoon into pie crust. Top with crumb
topping; sprinkle with cinnamon-sugar. Bake at 425 degrees for
50 minutes; sprinkle with additional cinnamon-sugar. Serves 6 to 8.

Crumb Topping:

1 c. all-purpose flour
1/2 c. brown sugar, packed

1/4 c. butter, chilled

Mix ingredients together until crumbly.

Give me juicy autumnal fruit ripe and red from the orchard.

-Walt Whitman

Honey-Custard Bread Pudding

Rogene Rogers
Bemidji, MN

Everyone is sure to enjoy this rich, old-fashioned bread pudding.

6 eggs, beaten
1/2 t. salt
4 c. milk
2/3 c. plus 2 T. honey, divided
2 T. butter, melted

Optional: 1/2 c. raisins
16-oz. loaf Vienna or
    French bread

Beat together eggs and salt in a small bowl; set aside. Bring milk just to a boil in a saucepan; let cool slightly. Stir 2/3 cup honey and butter into milk. Slowly stir eggs into milk mixture; add raisins, if using. Set aside. Tear bread into one-inch pieces and place in a greased 2-1/2 quart casserole dish. Pour egg mixture over bread. Place casserole dish in another larger pan and pour hot water into the pan to come halfway up the side of the dish. Bake at 325 degrees for one hour, or until set. About 15 minutes before serving, drizzle remaining honey over top. Makes 8 to 10 servings.

Gather bundles of fresh-from-the-garden herbs and tie with raffia. Add a little tag that you've written a friend's name on, to each bundle. A fragrant hostess gift and terrific way to use all the herbs still growing in your garden.

Orange Gingerbread

Carol Hickman
Kingsport, TN

A tasty combination of flavors that will get toes tapping!

1 c. shortening
1 c. brown sugar, packed
4 eggs, beaten
1 c. orange juice
1 c. molasses
3 c. all-purpose flour

2 t. baking powder
1 t. baking soda
1 t. salt
2 t. cinnamon
1-1/2 t. ground ginger
1 t. allspice

Blend together shortening and brown sugar in a large mixing bowl. Add eggs, mixing thoroughly; set aside. Heat orange juice and molasses in a small saucepan over medium-low heat, just until hot. Add to shortening mixture, stirring well to combine. Mix together remaining ingredients and add to shortening mixture, beating until smooth. Pour into a greased and floured 13"x9" baking pan. Bake at 325 degrees for 35 to 40 minutes. Cut into squares; spoon sauce over each serving. Makes 8 to 10 servings.

Sauce:

1/2 c. brown sugar, packed
1/4 c. butter

2 T. light corn syrup
1/2 t. vanilla extract

Combine brown sugar, butter and corn syrup in a small saucepan. Cook over medium-low heat, stirring constantly, until mixture comes to a boil. Boil for 2 minutes, stirring constantly. Remove from heat; stir in vanilla.

Pack school lunches filled with fun! Cut sandwiches into playful shapes and slide cheese cubes and fruit slices on a lollipop stick.

Butterscotch Bars

Judy Jones
Chinquapin, NC

*Wrap 'em up and set in a bowl by the door...friends & neighbors
will love taking this treat home.*

18-1/4 oz. spice or
   carrot cake mix
2 T. brown sugar, packed
1/2 c. oil
2 eggs

2 T. water
1/2 c. chopped walnuts
   or pecans
1 c. butterscotch chips

Stir together cake mix and brown sugar. Add oil, eggs and
water; mix well. Stir in nuts and butterscotch chips. Spread in a
13"x9" baking pan sprayed with non-stick vegetable spray. Bake
at 350 degrees until done but not dry, about 22 minutes. Let cool;
cut into bars. Makes 20 bars.

A little "magic" for the kids. Put a drop of green food coloring
into their milk glasses, then fill with milk as you tap the
glasses with a magic wand!

Frost on the Pumpkin Pie

Jean Cerutti
Kittanning, PA

*A frosty surprise for wee ones after an afternoon
spent jumping in leaves.*

1/4 c. margarine, melted
1-1/2 c. gingersnap
   cookies, crushed
15-oz. can pumpkin
1 pt. vanilla ice cream, softened

1 c. powdered sugar
1 t. pumpkin pie spice
8-oz. container frozen whipped
   topping, thawed

Stir margarine and cookie crumbs together; press into an ungreased
9" pie plate. Refrigerate. Combine pumpkin, ice cream and spice; blend
until smooth. Fold in whipped topping; pour into crust. Freeze for
several hours; let stand at room temperature for 20 to 25 minutes
before serving. Serves 8.

Roll silverware in dinner napkins, then wrap with bittersweet
vines or slip on a small grapevine wreath. A simple yet pretty
way to bring autumn to the table.

Pear Custard Bars

Kimberly Rockett
Fort Wayne, IN

A great way to ring in harvest season...very ripe fresh pears work well too.

1/2 c. butter, softened
1/3 c. plus 1/2 t. sugar, divided
3/4 c. all-purpose flour
1/4 t. vanilla extract
2/3 c. chopped pecans

15-1/4 oz. can pear halves, drained and sliced
1/4 t. cinnamon
1/4 t. nutmeg

Blend butter and 1/3 cup sugar in a mixing bowl. Stir in flour and vanilla until combined; add nuts. Press into a greased 8"x8" baking pan. Bake at 350 degrees for 20 minutes, or until golden; cool on a wire rack. Pour filling over baked crust. Arrange pear slices in a single layer over filling. Combine remaining sugar, cinnamon and nutmeg; sprinkle over pears. Raise oven temperature to 375 degrees; bake for 25 to 30 minutes. Center will be soft-set and become firmer upon cooling. Cool on a wire rack for 45 minutes; cover and refrigerate for at least 2 hours before cutting into bars. Store in refrigerator. Makes 16.

Filling:

8-oz. pkg. cream cheese, softened
1/2 c. sugar

1 egg
1/2 t. vanilla extract

Beat cream cheese in a bowl until smooth. Add sugar, egg and vanilla; mix until combined.

Buttery Maple-Walnut Drops

Ann Heavey
Bridgewater, MA

This recipe makes 4 dozen...just the right amount for a neighborhood tailgating party or harvest potluck.

2-1/4 c. all-purpose flour
1 t. baking soda
1 t. salt
1 c. butter, softened
3/4 c. sugar

3/4 c. brown sugar, packed
1-1/2 t. maple flavoring
2 eggs
1-1/2 c. chopped walnuts

Whisk flour, baking soda and salt in a small bowl; set aside. In another bowl, beat butter, sugars and maple flavoring until creamy; beat in eggs. Gradually add flour mixture and stir in walnuts. Drop by rounded tablespoonfuls onto ungreased baking sheets, placing about 1-1/2 inches apart. Bake at 375 degrees for 9 to 11 minutes. Makes 4 dozen.

Place family photos on a color copier and enlarge them to placemat size...sure to spark fun-filled conversations!

White Gingerbread

Marcia Marcoux
Charlton, MA

Although this recipe has no ginger in it, it's always been known by this name. It's great to enjoy on a brisk autumn day.

1 c. oil
2-1/3 c. sugar, divided
2 t. nutmeg
4 c. all-purpose flour
1/8 t. vanilla extract

1 t. salt
1 t. baking soda
1-1/3 c. buttermilk
Optional: whipped cream

Combine oil, 2 cups sugar and nutmeg in a large mixing bowl. Add flour, vanilla, salt, baking soda and buttermilk; blend well. Spread into a greased jelly-roll pan and sprinkle with remaining sugar. Bake at 350 degrees for 20 minutes, or until toothpick inserted near the center comes out clean. Serve plain or with a dollop of whipped cream. Makes 12 to 15 servings.

It's the perfect time of year to share some tasty treats with teachers, librarians and school bus drivers...let them know how much you appreciate them!

Pumpkin Trifle

Tina Abby
Carolina, RI

Very rich...an elegant treat with a cup of herbal tea.

14-1/2 oz. pkg. gingerbread
   cake mix
1-1/4 c. water
1 egg
4 c. milk
4 1-oz. pkgs. sugar-free instant
   butterscotch pudding mix

15-oz. can pumpkin
1 t. cinnamon
1/4 t. ground ginger
1/4 t. nutmeg
1/4 t. allspice
12-oz. container frozen
   whipped topping, thawed

Combine cake mix, water and egg in a mixing bowl. Mix well and pour into an ungreased 8"x8" baking pan. Bake at 350 degrees for 35 to 40 minutes, or until a toothpick inserted near the center comes out clean. Cool for 10 minutes; turn out of pan onto a wire rack. When completely cooled; crumble cake and set aside, reserving 1/4 cup crumbs for garnish. Whisk together milk and pudding mixes in a bowl for 2 minutes, or until slightly thickened. Let stand for 2 minutes, or until softly set. Stir in pumpkin and spices; mix well. In a trifle bowl or 3-1/2 quart glass serving bowl, layer one-quarter of the cake crumbs, one-half of pudding mixture, one-quarter of crumbs and one-half of whipped topping. Repeat layers, ending with topping. Garnish with reserved cake crumbs. Serve immediately or refrigerate. Serves 18.

'Tis the sweet, simple things of life
which are the real ones after all.

-Laura Ingalls Wilder

Double Delight Thumbprints

Mary Patenaude
Griswold, CT

Let the little ones make the thumbprints...Grandma will be tickled!

1/2 c. shortening
1/4 c. brown sugar, packed
1 egg, separated
1/2 t. vanilla extract
1/4 t. salt
1 c. all-purpose flour

1 c. pecans, finely chopped
14 caramels, unwrapped
3 T. whipping cream
1 c. milk chocolate chips
1 T. oil

Blend together shortening, brown sugar, egg yolk, vanilla and salt in a large bowl. Stir in flour; shape into one-inch balls. Dip balls in beaten egg white and roll in pecans. Arrange 2-inches apart on baking sheets; press thumb gently into center to make a deep indentation. Bake at 375 degrees for 12 to 14 minutes, or until golden. Cool on a wire rack. Stir caramels and whipping cream together in a small saucepan over low heat, until melted and smooth. Spoon caramel mixture by 1/2 teaspoonfuls into cookie indentations; let cool. Place chocolate chips and oil in a microwave-safe container. Microwave on high setting, stirring until smooth; drizzle over cookies. Makes 2 dozen.

Need a family night sweet treat in just seconds? Combine candy corn with nuts...yummy!

Gail's Pumpkin Bars

Lisa Thomsen
Rapid City, SD

A super dessert to make in the fall. After baking and frosting you can go ahead and freeze them for the holidays!

4 eggs, beaten
1 c. oil
2 c. sugar
15-oz. can pumpkin
2 c. all-purpose flour
2 t. baking powder

1 t. baking soda
1/2 t. salt
2 t. cinnamon
1/2 t. ground ginger
1/2 t. nutmeg
1/2 t. ground cloves

Mix together eggs, oil, sugar and pumpkin in a large bowl. Add remaining ingredients and mix well; pour into a greased and floured 18"x12" jelly-roll pan. Bake at 350 degrees for 30 to 40 minutes, until a toothpick comes out clean. Let cool; frost and cut into bars. Makes 1-1/2 to 2 dozen.

Cream Cheese Frosting:

8-oz. pkg. cream cheese, softened
6 T. butter, softened

1 T. milk
1 t. vanilla extract
4 c. powdered sugar

Beat together cream cheese, butter, milk and vanilla; stir in powdered sugar to a spreading consistency.

For a fall fragrance, burn candles in warm scents such as spiced pear, cinnamon or baked apple.

Index

Appetizers

Antipasto, 66
Apple & Brie Toasts, 68
Artichoke-Garlic Dip, 71
Autumn Harvest Fruit Dip, 59
Buffalo Wing Chip Dip, 70
Cheddar Cheese Ball, 55
Cheesy Fruit & Nut Spread, 59
Cranberry-Almond Crunch Mix, 62
Creamy Apple Cider Dip, 63
Frosted Pecans, 75
Ghostly Party Dip, 58
Glazed Cocktail Sausages, 140
Harvest Moon Caramel Corn, 72
Herb-Seasoned Spinach Balls, 64
Hot Bacon & Swiss Dip, 61
Howling Good Snack Mix, 72
Italian Meatballs, 67
Maple-Topped Sweet Potato Skins, 69
Oh-So-Cheesy Chili Dip, 57
Old-Fashioned Kettle Corn, 74
Oniony Crab Dip, 140
Pear & Blue Cheese Crostini, 76
Philly Dip, 66
Pizza Fondue, 141
Pumpkin Cheese Ball, 58
Queso Blanco, 60
Sausage-Sauerkraut Balls, 65
Scrumptious Stuffed Potato Skins, 54
Shoo Vampire Garlic Spread, 56
Sweet & Spicy Pecans, 73
Taco Joe Dip, 141
Tailgating Tortilla Wrap-Ups, 70
Texas 2-Step Guacamole, 71
Thanksgiving Harvest Mix, 74
White Chocolate Party Mix, 75

Breads

Autumn Spice Bread, 118
Bacon-Cheese Muffins, 130
Butterscotch Bread, 133
Coffee Can Pumpkin Bread, 114
Corny Cornbread, 129
Cranberry-Buttermilk Bread, 111
Fiesta Cornbread, 122
Mini Pumpkin Loaves, 125
Patchwork Muffins, 132
Pecan Pie Mini Muffins, 115
Raisin-Berry Bread, 119
Rosemary Crisp Bread, 121
Soft Gingerbread, 118
Sour Cream Biscuits, 131
Super-Simple Bread Bowls, 116

Beverages

Amaretto Tea, 16
Apple Dapple Punch, 20
Bewitching Brew, 13
Chai Tea, 137
Cinnamon-Maple Nog, 6
Citrus Slush, 15
Cranberry Slush, 21
Creamy Sweet Almond Milk, 8
Fall Harvest Warmer, 10
Fireside Sipper, 7
French Hot Chocolate, 12
Frosty Fall Punch, 14
Fruity Spiced Tea, 18
Hot Caramel Apple Cider, 136
Hot Chocolate Supreme, 8
Hot Spicy Cider for a Crowd, 136
Lemony Ginger Tea, 11
Maple Cream Coffee Creamer, 9
Mexican Hot Chocolate, 22
Minty Hot Cocoa, 23
Mocha Coffee Mix, 9
Old-Fashioned Hot Chocolate, 17
Razzleberry Tea, 24
Russian Tea Mix, 14
Spicy Citrus Cider, 6
Sweater Weather Tea, 19

Breakfasts

Apple & Raisin Oatmeal, 33
Apple Scones, 42
Apple-Waffle Sandwiches, 47
Autumn Pancakes, 49
Bacon & Egg Filled Tomatoes, 45

Index

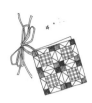

Best-Ever Sticky Buns, 37
Breakfast Apple Cobbler, 138
Cheesy Bacon Casserole, 30
Cheesy Breakfast Casserole, 139
Chocolatey Gingerbread Waffles, 28
Country Breakfast Sandwiches, 46
Country Morning Bacon Muffins, 51
Crispy Home Fries, 41
Crunchy Coconut Granola, 139
Devonshire Cream, 42
Fall Harvest French Toast, 26
Farmhouse Favorite Sausage, 31
Fruit & Nut Bread, 48
Gingerbread Pancakes, 43
Grandmommy's Casserole, 35
Herbed Quiche, 44
Maple-Sausage Breakfast Casserole, 29
Mom's Instant Coffee Bars, 52
Nutty Pecan Popovers, 32
Omelets in a Bag, 40
Pumpkin Pancakes, 27
Reuben Brunch Bake, 38
Rise & Shine Quiche, 50
Savory Breakfast Pancakes, 34
Sugary Cinnamon Roll-Ups, 36
Texas-Style Breakfast Casserole, 39
Warm & Cozy Oatmeal, 138

Desserts

Apple Crunch Pie, 209
Butterscotch Bars, 212
Buttery Maple-Walnut Drops, 215
Caramel Flan, 199
Cinnamon Flop Cake, 201
Cinnamon Jumbles, 207
Creamy Pumpkin Fudge, 205
Double Delight Thumbprints, 218
Dutch Nutmeg Cookies, 203
Frost on the Pumpkin Pie, 213
Gail's Pumpkin Bars, 219
Ginger-Pumpkin Mousse, 195
Golden Peach Cobbler, 161
Harvest Celebration Cake, 194
Honey-Custard Bread Pudding, 210

Honey-Pumpkin Pie, 208
Mini Maple-Pear Cobblers, 206
Nutty Chocolate Fudge, 160
Orange Gingerbread, 211
Pear Custard Bars, 214
Pulled Molasses Taffy, 204
Pumpkin Bread Pudding, 196
Pumpkin Pie Cake, 200
Pumpkin Sandwich Cookies, 202
Pumpkin Trifle, 217
Sweet Potato Pound Cake, 197
Triple Chocolate Cake, 162
Turtle Cookies, 198
White Gingerbread, 216

Mains

Apple-Glazed Pork Roast, 153
Autumn Pork with Apple Chutney, 164
Autumn Supper Chicken, 148
Bacon-Mushroom Spaghetti Pie, 191
Baked Steak with Gravy, 188
Beef Paprika, 157
Buttermilk Chicken, 180
Chicken Noodle Casserole, 189
Chicken Tetrazzini, 174
Chicken-Netti, 155
Chill Chaser Chili Bake, 179
Cranberry Pot Roast, 165
Creamy Shrimp Fettuccine, 176
Dutch Spareribs & Dumplings, 154
Farmhouse Pork & Sauerkraut, 149
Garlic Pot Roast, 181
Hearty Red Beans & Rice, 171
Homestyle Meatloaf, 190
Italian 3-Cheese Stuffed Shells, 175
Italian Chicken, 159
Italian Chicken & Artichokes, 177
Italian-Style French Dip, 157
Martelli Pasta Gravy, 170
Mom's Sicilian Pot Roast, 187
New England Turkey & Stuffing, 169
Old-Fashioned Chicken Pot Pie, 172
Parmesan Pork Chop Bake, 173
Penne & Sausage, 183

Index

Praline Mustard-Glazed Ham, 168
Roast Turkey with Sage Butter, 166
Roasted Turkey Breast, 156
Savory Low Country Shrimp & Grits, 158
Southwestern Casserole, 178
Steak & Spinach Pinwheels, 184
Stuffed Cabbage Rolls, 182
Sunday Chicken & Dressing, 167
Super-Easy Stuffed Peppers, 192
Super-Simple Lasagna, 186
Tarragon Chicken, 185

Sides

Apple & Cranberry Sauce, 83
Bacon-Topped Veggie Bake, 106
Best-Ever Onion Casserole, 107
Candied-Glazed Baked Apples, 80
Caramel Apple Salad, 83
Carrots Au Gratin, 87
Cauliflower Au Gratin, 93
Cheddar-Colby Pasta Bake, 86
Cheesy Rice & Veggies, 95
Corn Soufflé, 82
Cornmeal Dumplings, 84
Country-Style Bean Bake, 106
Country-Style Ham Au Gratin, 150
Cranberries & Spinach Salad, 100
Cranberry-Yam Bake, 79
Creamed Spinach Casserole, 88
Creamy Butternut Squash, 81
Deliciously Cheesy Potatoes, 142
French-Style Green Bean Bake, 103
Garlic & Herb Mashed Potatoes, 104
Golden Cornbread Dressing, 91
Golden Homestyle Rice, 108
Ham & Lima Bean Pot, 102
Hearty Macaroni & Cheese, 85
Homestyle Cornbread Dressing, 144
Honey-Kissed Acorn Squash, 97
Indian Summer Rice, 151
Jalapeño-Cheese Rice, 104
Loaded Mashed Potato Casserole, 92
Maple-Glazed Carrots, 78

Mary's Nutty Greek Salad, 101
Mashed Cinnamon Sweet Potatoes, 99
Mom's Cranberry Salad, 101
Mom's Sausage Dressing, 98
Nut & Honey Potato Salad, 82
Nutty Sweet Potatoes, 143
Old-Fashioned Cheese Bake, 89
Saucy Red Beans, 145
Scalloped Apples, 96
Scalloped Oyster Stuffing, 94
Sour Cream Potatoes, 90
Spicy Fruit & Bread Stuffing, 96
Sweet Potato Salad, 105

Soups

Bacon-Corn Chowder, 150
Broccoli-Cheese Soup, 131
Chicken & Dumpling Soup, 112
Chicken Fajita Chowder, 123
Curried Pumpkin Soup, 127
Easy as A, B, Seafood Bisque, 117
Farmers' Market Stew, 152
Garlicky Chicken Stew, 147
Halloween Soup, 130
Northern Sausage Soup, 146
Old-Fashioned Split Pea Soup, 134
Prize-Winning Chili, 128
Smoked Sausage Potato Soup, 126
Smokey Hollow Vegetable Soup, 124
Spanish Rice Soup, 120
White Bean, Pasta & Sausage Soup, 120
Winter Warm-Up Beef Simmer, 113
Woods Creek Bean Soup, 110

We've cooked up a whole collection of *Gooseberry Patch*® books!

Have a taste for more? Call us toll-free at
1-800-854-6673
We'll send you our latest catalog filled with kitchenware, candles, handmade quilts, gourmet goodies, enamelware, bowls, bubble night lights and our very own line of cookbooks, calendars and organizers!

Phone us:
1·800·854·6673

Fax us:
1·740·363·7225

Visit our website:
www.gooseberrypatch.com

Send us your favorite recipe!

and the memory that makes it special for you!* If we select your recipe for a brand new **Gooseberry Patch** cookbook, your name will appear right along with it...and you'll receive a FREE copy of the book! Mail to:

Gooseberry Patch
Attn: Book Dept.
P.O. Box 190
Delaware, OH 43015

*Please include the number of servings and all other necessary information!

bonfires russet red leaves

wagon rides

Thanksgiving memories

family gatherings

crackling fires

comfort food pumpkin patch

U.S. to Canadian recipe equivalents

Volume Measurements

1/4 teaspoon	1 mL
1/2 teaspoon	2 mL
1 teaspoon	5 mL
1 tablespoon = 3 teaspoons	15 mL
2 tablespoons = 1 fluid ounce	30 mL
1/4 cup	60 mL
1/3 cup	75 mL
1/2 cup = 4 fluid ounces	125 mL
1 cup = 8 fluid ounces	250 mL
2 cups = 1 pint =16 fluid ounces	500 mL
4 cups = 1 quart	1 L

Weights

1 ounce	30 g
4 ounces	120 g
8 ounces	225 g
16 ounces = 1 pound	450 g

Oven Temperatures

300° F	150° C
325° F	160° C
350° F	180° C
375° F	190° C
400° F	200° C
450° F	230° C

Baking Pan Sizes

Square

8x8x2 inches	2 L = 20x20x5 cm
9x9x2 inches	2.5 L = 23x23x5 cm

Rectangular

13x9x2 inches	3.5 L = 33x23x5 cm

Loaf

9x5x3 inches	2 L = 23x13x7 cm

Round

8x1-1/2 inches	1.2 L = 20x4 cm
9x1-1/2 inches	1.5 L = 23x4 cm